I0235193

TELLUSIAN SEED

by
Mark A. Carter

Copyright © 2011 by Mark A. Carter. All Rights Reserved.
ISBN: 978-0-9810585-2-8

Registered with the Canadian ISBN Service System
(CISS) – Library and Archives Canada.

First Hardcover Printing October 2014

Visit the author's website at: http://markacarter.com.

Mark A. Carter Publications
Windsor, Ontario, CANADA
e-mail: markacarter@yahoo.ca

Also from the imagination of Mark A. Carter:
  Hephzibah of Heaven
  Thea of The Seraphim

This novel is dedicated to Gerry Simmons, 63: 7 heart attacks, 4 strokes, 6 heart surgeries, 7 back operations, and 27 major surgeries, a humble man recovering from a full knee replacement who occupied the bed beside me at WRH-Met while I put the finishing touches on *Tellusian Seed*, who believes that he is one of God's helpers, who like Saint Francis of Assisi feeds the birds and the squirrels, and who considers every trial of Job that he has endured as merely a bump in the road.

A rough road leads to the stars.
An even rougher road leads to God.

foreword

I have been blessed by several encounters with Angels during the course of my life. The first encounter scared me to death. The second and third were miracles. And the fourth took my breath away.

When I was five years old, I got up in the middle of the night to go pee. But when I got to the washroom I encountered an Angel in full body armor standing in the center of the room. The deific creature terrified me. I stepped backwards, exited the room, and assembled a brick wall of facial tissue boxes, with a thought, in the open doorway. Then I ran back to my bedroom, shut the door which was usually left open, hid beneath the covers, and fell asleep once again, assuming that I was awake to start with. For most of my life I assumed that the experience was little more than a fanciful dream. Upon reflection, I'm not so sure.

My second encounter occurred when I was nine. I fell out of the upper branches of the pear tree in my back yard, on a particularly windy day, when I should have known better. But the tree and I were inseparable. And I was just a monkey boy swinging away in the upper branches and enjoying the wild ride that day. When my grip came loose and I fell the fifteen feet to the ground I should have hit a couple of major limbs on the way down. I should have landed hard and broken something. I should have had the wind knocked out of me, at least. But none of that happened. Time seemed to pass slowly as I fell. And I landed as light as a feather. It was as if I was gripped by some unknown force and placed on the ground carefully. It shocked me when it happened. And it still haunts me. I consider it a personal miracle. And I am convinced that an Angel who I could not see was behind it.

Tellusian Seed by Mark Carter

A second miracle occurred just after supper one day in late fall when I was eleven years old. My dad had bundled us all into the old two-tone Buick that he drove and took us across town to visit my aunt and uncle. When we got there, I discovered that my uncle had taken off for his post prandial walk. I got permission to go with him, and hurried out of the house. In order to follow him, I had to cross Glenridge Avenue, a busy street. I stood at the crosswalk and waited for the light to change. When it did, I stepped off the curb. But I was pulled back forcefully, by the collar. I said, "Hey." Then the Doppler wail of a blaring horn hit me, as a car running the red light on my side surged past inches from me. And I realized immediately that someone had saved me from certain injury and perhaps even death by pulling me back. And I was grateful. But when I turned around to thank my benefactor, there was nobody there.

But the most remarkable encounter with an Angel occurred while Donna and I were shopping at the Tecumseh Mall. As we entered the department store a beautiful girl walked past me from right to left and came to a stop with her back to me. She was tall and elegant with long black hair. And I recognized her immediately. Donna walked ahead, but I was stopped in my tracks by the girl because I sensed that she was an Angel. Moreover, she was the Angel who I had seen in dreams throughout my life, always standing shoulder to shoulder with me, on my left side. I knew her as a friend and benefactor, with a sense of humor, who put up with my bad jokes and ceaseless elbowing. When she turned and smiled at me, it took my breath away. I smiled back. I stared into her face for a moment, then looked away because, in the waking realm, she was too much to behold. One of the hardest things I have ever had to do was to leave her that day and search for Donna. But I did. I sensed that it was not my time to be with the Angel. So I caught up with Donna and we did our shopping. I told her of the encounter when we got home and had our evening tea. And she shared the story with me of a similar encounter she had experienced years before with an Angel seen sitting in a passing car.

I firmly believe that Angels and other sub-deities from their realm exist all around us, either invisibly like the Angels who visit me when I pray and write or visibly like the Angels my wife and I saw and sensed. Open your eyes and your hearts and you shall sense or even see them too. They are everywhere. You will always know them by the emotional response they elicit in you. Their beauty will take your breath away. As for me, I can't help but weep in their presence.

Listen to "You're Beautiful" by James Blunt from his *Back to Bedlam* CD from Atlantic Records to experience his emotional reaction to an Angel, for a moment, on the subway.

The previous encounters that I had, as a child, convinced me to write *Hephzibah of Heaven* and *Thea of the Seraphim*. They have filled me with awe and wonder for a very long time. But it was my fourth encounter with the Angel that I saw that inspired me to write *Tellusian Seed*. The moment that I had with her was yet another verification of the divine in our midst. And if I never see another Angel for the rest of my life, the moment I had with her will have to suffice.

TELLUSIAN SEED

Chapter 1 - dawn

Asmooth, polished wall of red granite stood upon the outcrop above the first encampment of the New Earth. The wall was oriented so that the first orange rays of spring caught its inward edge and reflected sunlight into a circular grove of trees below. The stone was inscribed with the names of Noah's entire crew, with special annotations for Lily, Rose, Shepherd, and Violet.

The memorial told the story about the destruction of Earth, of Noah's journey through space and time, and of the reseeding of the planet. The memorial spoke of the New Earth. It was a name none of the inhabitants currently used to describe their world. The Earth had been renamed Tellus Mater. It meant Mother Earth. In ancient Greek, it was Gaea. The inhabitants called themselves Tellusians.

The Illuminati of the old world had tried to corrupt the New Earth with supermen and superwomen of genetic manufacture designed to be faster, stronger, and taller through the controlled breeding of Olympians. These Alpha creatures would control the New Earth. They would be in charge of the lesser human beings, the mongrels, the Shepherds.

To the Illuminati, only physicality, power, and vicious intelligence were important. Spirituality was irrelevant. So, when Diana cherished the spirits of Lily, Rose, and Shepherd above all, the plans of the Illuminati were thrown into a tailspin. After centuries of controlled breeding, education, and investment, the Illuminati ended up backing the wrong horse. The supermen they created fell by the wayside, and the meek, the mongrels, the physically inferior but spiritually superior prevailed. Literally, as had been foretold, the meek inherited the New Earth.

Tellusian Seed by Mark Carter

The meek of the world reborn embraced an agrarian culture
modeled after how Hephzibah described the day-to-day farm life of
Heaven. The Heaven on Earth created by the Tellusians was filled with
apple orchards, planted in the name of the Mother, and in remembrance
of Shepherd; flax, so the daughters could weave linen and make
clothes; olive trees, so they could have oil; cypress trees, so they could
have shade on hot summer days; rye, so they could bake bread; and
sunflowers, in remembrance of the Son and his sacrifice.

Beside the red granite memorial was a podium made of mahogany
set up for the occasion. Standing behind the podium was Lily's
daughter. Her name was Eve, and she was ten thousand years old. She
looked out over an apple orchard so vast that it stretched to the horizon.

Directly in front of the memorial was the sacred grove, small now in
comparison to the edifices built over the years, decades, centuries, and
millennia by the Daughters of Tellus Mater. On both sides of the grove
were rows of chairs. One hundred thousand chairs were filled with
generations of daughters dressed in ecru linen blouses, dark brown
linen dresses, and cobbled shoes. They were there on that day of
commemoration, straw hats in hand, to listen to Eve's message for her
time among them was coming to an end.

"Sisters," said the stentorian voice of the diaphanous creature at the
podium, "welcome."

The transcended daughter of Lily stood at the podium as an
ephemeral creature of yellow light. Diaphanous, ethereal, and elegant,
Eve was the bridge between the deities who resided within the grove
and the Daughters of Tellus Mater. She was the high-priestess. She
took over where Lily left off.

Eve was interrupted by the morning song of a robin. She paused out
of respect for its six hundred and fifty million year heritage, while the
orange-breasted raptor sang its song of joy at the dawn of the new day.
The audience listened, as well, to the song of the feathered dinosaur
that lived among them. The robin's song was a celebration of life, a
celebration of the morning, and like the Daughters of Tellus Mater and
the Angels in Heaven, it was given up to God as a prayer. Being so,
the ancient creature with a winged lineage going back to Archaeopteryx
was highly respected and revered by the Tellusians.

The robin finished its song and flew away to sing from a different
location, and Eve resumed.

Chapter 1 - dawn

She smiled at the Daughters of Tellus Mater, and they smiled back. Everyone understood the symbolism behind the robin's song, and was moved. The song was a blessing from the oldest surviving creature of the old Earth, brought through space and time aboard Noah, to the newly evolved and transformed inhabitants of the New Earth.

"I meet with you here," said Eve, "on this special occasion, to commemorate the ten thousand year anniversary of our arrival on the New Earth. We have come far, in a short span of time, and should be proud of ourselves. We have built cities that honor the Mother. We live lives that honor the Mother. Now, at this point in our societal and spiritual evolution, we embark into the galaxy that we call home to spread the Word of the Mother."

The audience clapped exuberantly.

Eve raised her right hand to quiet her sisters.

"Praise God the Mother," said Eve, "from which all blessings flow."

"Praise God," said one hundred thousand voices, in response.

"Let me quote," said Eve, "from the *Book of Gabriel.*"

One hundred thousand Tellusians bowed their heads, in veneration.

"Listen to me," quoted Eve, "for I am Gabriel. God Almighty is in my pen. The Mother of Creation is in my pen. The Son is in my pen. And the Trinity spoke to me as the One in three voices: that of an old man, an old woman, and a young man. And God said:

> Believe in me, for I believe in you.
> Respect life,
> for life is the greatest gift I can bestow.
> Love God, for you are loved by God,
> and held in esteem above the highest Angels.
>
> Do good, for the sake of the Father.
> Love one another, for the sake of the Son.
> Help one another, for the sake of the Mother.
> BE, for the sake of the Daughter,
> and let destiny unfold.

Sisters," continued Eve, "on this bright, spring morning, we do great good. Today, we launch a thousand starships into space, each headed for a solar system we know to be inhabited by intelligent life. We go to spread the Word of the Mother throughout the Milky Way. We journey forth to spread her words of love and of peace. Soon, a new day shall dawn across our galaxy."

The audience clapped.

"Aboard those thousand starships," said Eve, "we disperse ten thousand of our newly transcended sisters. We throw this seed of Tellus Mater, this Tellusian seed, into the cosmos, like sowing a field in springtime, in the hope that some will take root and flourish. We wish them well. We love them and shall miss them. I ask you to stand, and to chant our sacred mantra given to us in the *Book of Gabriel*, as the starships are launched."

One hundred thousand daughters stood up.

One thousand starships launched.

The Daughters of Tellus Mater pointed to the sky, following the starships with their fingertips, as the vessels seared upward through the atmosphere. Behind the electromagnetic roar of the launches was the sound of a deep, throbbing mantra. The rising, octaval chant of one hundred thousand daughters of Tellus filled the air of the cool, spring day with Gabriel's joyous words of salvation. "I'm CLEAN," sang the female voices. "Just BEEE."

Chapter 2 - lenses

The starships that launched the Tellusian missionaries into space to spread the Word of the Mother through the *Book of Gabriel* among the stars of the Milky Way galaxy were themselves living creatures of a kind. They were living starships woven from the fabric of energy itself. And like the Tellusians, they had evolved from the corporeal to mostly ethereal over time.

The starships were a gift from Hephzibah. She introduced the Tellusians to living, sentient beings who once swam, as tiny creatures, in the tepid sea of a far off world and resembled cuttlefish who had evolved, had journeyed into space, and had become behemoths. Where once they looked upward and viewed the night sky with stars circling overhead, they now journeyed among them.

The twinkling stars called to them for millions of years. God, as they knew him, called to them. They yearned to be among the stars and closer to their creator. They instinctively sensed it was where they belonged. They imagined themselves traveling among the suns. And when they became mentally strong enough, they thought themselves into space in a quest to find their creator, in a quest to find God.

These sentient creatures had metamorphosed from tiny intelligent sea creatures into space behemoths, into living starships. Whereas they once communicated with each other by flashing their thoughts across the surface of their skin in rapid, colorful pulses and patterns, they now talked telepathically. Although, when their emotions got the better of them, they still lit up like Christmas trees in the deep blackness of space, which startled their fellow travelers and themselves and was much cause for embarrassment and lighthearted ridicule. Millions of years ago, when they thrived in a tepid, salt water sea, they feasted on shrimp-like creatures. Now they fed off of the cosmic radiation emitted by the stars themselves.

When they heard Hephzibah calling to them across space and time, they journeyed to Tellus Mater, thinking that they had found God. Hephzibah explained to them that it was the Father who had sowed the seeds of cold life among the stars. But it was the Mother who was the Master Creator. It was the Mother who had created the Father, the Son, her sister Seraphim, and herself. It was not her. It was not Hephzibah. She was merely a Seraph, a Princess of Heaven, and the Goddess of a small water world. As much as they were disappointed, the living starships were also overjoyed to know that there was indeed a God, a Trinity of Gods, and that they were on the right path to find them.

Hephzibah introduced the space behemoths to the Tellusians who were also on a path to God. The giant creatures sensed that the Daughters of Tellus Mater were kindred spirits. Moreover, they sensed that the evolved humans had something that they needed and needed something that they had. So, the tentacled giants formed a symbiotic relationship with the Tellusians, and became devoted to them.

These living ships called themselves Lenses, which in their telepathic language meant *Dancers in the Stream*. They called themselves Lenses because it defined what they did and who they were. Where once they swam in the warm, aquamarine sea of their home world, using squirts of water and undulations of fragile fins to move, they now danced in the frigid darkness of space and journeyed from star to star with undulations of their thoughts. They traveled through space, in pods, resembling gigantic whales now more than cuttlefish, swimming in the magnetic stream between suns where they were squeezed by gravitational lensing, curved through space and time, and surged to their next destination. But the Tellusians called them Utera in their language, and gave each Utera a name.

Although the name Utera was distinctively female, in the Tellusian tongue, and meant egg, the Daughters of Tellus Mater had a compulsion to give each Utera a male name to keep track of them officially. They gave them the names of heroes from out of old Earth history. They bestowed upon the eggs the names of artists, poets, and philosophers. After being without men for ten thousand years, the Tellusians developed a romanticized notion of men, although men had subjugated women throughout history, been their undoing, and were considered to be evil by the Mother of Creation herself.

The Utera, on the other hand, had their own names for themselves and their kind. And these were the names that their Tellusian symbiotes knew them by when they spoke with them. And all of their names ended with *sha* which meant *of God*, in their language.

So, a thousand starships were injected into the great swirl. But their destinies depended on where they went. To some of the aliens that the Tellusians encountered, they were salvation. To others, they were manna from Heaven. To the rest, they were anathema.

This is the story of three Utera of the thousand that departed Tellus Mater on that special spring day on their journey to vastly different worlds among the stars. It is the story of Utera Davidos or Xuxa and the Gabrielican Sisters of Atonement who journeyed to the icy moon Lesta and were embraced with benevolence. It is the story of Utera Kutuzov or Misha and the Daughters of Tellus Mater who journeyed within her to the swamp planet Alterna and were confronted with ambivalence. And it is the story of Utera Lysanderos or Deesha and her precious cargo of missionaries who journeyed to the oil-rich desert planet Rancor and encountered malevolence.

Moreover, it is the story about the Daughters left behind on Mother Earth. It is a story about the birth of an Angel, about the miraculous creation of the first god outside of Heaven, and about God Almighty finally forgiving us all. It is a story about Tellus Mater becoming the center of the seventh universe. And, in the end, when all is said and done, it is ultimately the story about the merciful dissolution of the Chorus, God, and Paradise itself into the cobalt blue, Celestial Sea from which all things come and eventually go. And then …

Chapter 3 - rim

Utera Davidos was a living starship. She was partly there but sometimes not, and usually ethereal but often corporeal as she swam the cold, galactic sea from star to star much as her ancestors once swam the warm, tropical waters of her home world. But now, she was no longer fragile, small and tentacled. She was a lucid behemoth whose skin contained zwitterion molecules that vacillated their charge with her every conscious thought much as the skin of her ancestors displayed, in flashes of color and pattern, what was on their minds when they were cuttlefish. And so, her negatively charged body was attracted by the positive charge of a star. It pulled her to it. And when she got close, she flipped her charge to match the sun's and was electromagnetically repelled by the like charge and flung to her next solar stepping stone *en route* to God. But for now, she and her precious Tellusian cargo were headed for Lesta and would soon be there.

Utera Davidos called herself Xuxa which, despite its spelling, was pronounced *Shu Sha* and meant Shu of God. Shu itself, in the telepathic Uteran language was a soft sounding and soothing name reflecting her usual demeanor and personality, and meant *light sparkling on the sea at sunrise* or Day Sea. The Tellusians had a similar name for Day Sea and called many of their children Dagmar.

Since meeting the Tellusians, becoming immersed in their culture, viewing the biodiversity on their world, and being told the names for most things, the Utera affectionately teased Xuxa with a similar sounding name to her own. In their thoughts, they imagined a field of short, white-flowered, herbaceous weeds with creeping rhizomes and spoon-shaped evergreen leaves called *Bellis perennis*. Although the flowers appeared yellow centered with white petals, each petal was an individual flower. And so, the archetypal species of that name represented more than mere flowers to the Uteras. It became a symbol of many in one and one amid many, and conjured images of schools of cuttlefish swimming in an ancient sea, and Utera swimming light years apart but in telepathic contact with each other amid the stars of the Milky Way. And so, Day Sea took on a revered meaning among them. And when the Uteras wished to talk to her, they projected the image of yellow florets surrounded by white rays across the vast distances at the speed of thought. And she heard them. Although her name was Day Sea of God, her Uteran sisters nicknamed her Daisy.

To the casual observer, if there was such a thing in the deep darkness of space between suns, Xuxa appeared to be a rogue object, at first blush, perhaps an asteroid or a comet. But on closer inspection, the burnt umber ovoid hurdling through the void at tremendous velocity was not twisting, turning and tumbling, as most natural objects did. It was smooth, not pockmarked with astroblemes, and looked like burnished brass. It seemed to be under control. The observer would conclude that there was intelligence behind her movement, that the object itself was man-made although not necessarily made by man, that it was a starship. But the observer would be right and wrong. Although Xuxa traveled at the velocity of some advanced space vehicles and appeared to be a starship, she was not. She was a living sentient creature who lived in deep space, fed off of gamma rays, had befriended the Tellusians, had entered into a devoted symbiotic relationship with them, and only behaved like a starship when in the mood to do so.

Xuxa considered what the casual observer might make of her as she journeyed through the void and changed her outward appearance randomly just to mystify anyone in the galaxy who might be looking her way. She might appear to be a golden egg, then apparently disappear, sending a charge through herself to invoke electromagnetically induced transparency, a throwback to when her ancestors lived in the sea. She might turn white, gray or black. She might turn iridescent green, shimmering, or fluorescent. And just for the sake of change, just for the Hell of it, just because she had a picosecond of whimsy, Xuxa might transform her outer skin into an iridescent spectrum of oil in a puddle, refracting star light in a thousand spectral swirls.

While Xuxa amused herself with cosmetic frivolities during the long journey between stars, her precious cargo slept through the dark night within their stasis chambers deep within her. Xuxa's interior was devoid of features, curved, smooth, and seamless, in its default form, much like the empty shell of an egg. There was no cockpit with controls, cargo bay, or air lock. There was no intercom to communicate within the ship or radio and antenna to communicate with the outside world. There were no lights to illuminate her interior, or antigravity plating to hold her passengers from floating freely. There was no life support system regulating atmospheric gases, pressure, and temperature. There was no visible technology at all. Yet, it was there within her. And she could transform herself, with a thought, to be as complex or as simple as the Tellusians required. They were her symbiotes, her companions, her charges. She was devoted to them and to their care. And she would let nothing befall them.

Xuxa's sleeping Tellusian symbiotes traveled with her and within her, sealed securely inside cryogenic chambers, and tucked safely within her throbbing, organic walls. She monitored their status once per minute. Adjustments were performed once an hour. She was mother to them. She was womb. And they were her children.

When Xuxa first detected the dim, planetary twinkle coming from the outer planets, the gas giants of the Angel system, everyone aboard Utera Davidos was asleep. The sleeping occupants, Tellusian missionaries to a strange world, like their symbiotic partner and host who enveloped them and transported them across the galaxy, were more energy than matter, more ethereal than corporeal. Yet the vast distance of the voyage forced even them to rest in stasis chambers to let the passage of time stream over them unnoticed.

When Xuxa determined that they were near enough to their destination, at their current velocity, she awakened the Tellusian ambassador, as per her instructions. Her name was Athena. She had asked to be awakened when they neared the Oort cloud of the Angel system; in order to get a head's up, as she put it. And they were indeed there. So Xuxa filled the interior of the starship, her interior, with breathable gases, and heated herself to a range within which her fragile Daughters of Tellus Mater could function. While Athena and her Tellusian sisters slumbered, Xuxa had evacuated and reabsorbed the atmospheric gases from her interior and had let her core temperature drop to that of the interstellar cold as she traversed the space between stars. Xuxa had mentioned the procedure to Athena before the flight, and the Tellusian understood. She had commented that it was like turning off a light bulb when leaving a room. She understood that Xuxa was simply being efficient. Now Xuxa optimized her interior for Tellusian life support and flooded herself with seventy-eight percent nitrogen, twenty-one percent oxygen, and point zero four percent carbon dioxide at fourteen point seven pounds per square inch and sixty-eight degrees Fahrenheit. And when everything was right, she awakened Athena from cryogenic stasis.

"Let there be light," said Xuxa's calm, female voice amid the darkness within her that was far more absolute than the blackness of the interstellar night and utterly devoid of even the faintest star light. And a localized light illuminated a spot of the interior of the empty egg transforming that spot instantly from featureless black to orange, and revealing the mental projection of Utera Davidos, the three dimensional embodiment of Xuxa herself standing in the center of the light, like an actor standing in a spotlight upon her curved, inner surface.

Xuxa's mental projection was feminine, tall and ethereal, with fiery-orange hair held back and tied with a golden braid. She was dressed in a diaphanous, ankle length gown of fluorescent green tied around her waist with a bright red bow. On her feet, she wore golden sandals. And for all intents and purposes, she was Tellusian.

Xuxa had been in contact with many species during her voyage through the galaxy and she had changed her mental projection to match each species. It was far easier for sentient creatures to form a symbiotic relationship with her if she, in part, looked like them. So, despite her actual enormous size and shape, which the aliens were always aware of, Utera Davidos always looked somewhat like them in their minds, in a strange sort of duality. For the present, her mental projection was Tellusian because she was bonded to Tellusians. And, in doing so, and in adapting to them and in adopting their thinking and their extended belief in God, she was more of a friend to them than a newcomer, and more of a sister to them than merely organic technology, than merely a creature who served as a living starship.

Xuxa raised her right arm ever so slightly and moved her hand in a graceful outward curve. And in doing so, Athena materialized. She metamorphosed from transparency to opacity upon a scarlet chaise longue within her stasis chamber, and opened her eyes. Athena's large, ovoid, milky blue eyes looked at Xuxa with the true affection of a sister. And Athena asked, "Have we arrived?"

"Not yet, Mother," said Xuxa respectfully.

Athena stretched her back like a cat, rose, stepped toward Xuxa, wrapped her arms around her, and hugged her with genuine affection. Then Athena pulled back with her hands on Xuxa's shoulders, and asked, "Where are we?"

"We have reached the outer rim of the Angel system," said Xuxa. "Braking has begun. You ordered me to awaken you ahead of the others."

"Excellent," replied her enthusiastic symbiote. "Let's have a look."

The mental projection of the starship and the Tellusian ambassador to Celeste stepped toward the curved wall of the featureless interior. Meanwhile, behind them, where the chaise longue had extended out of the floor, the ship sucked it back. The matter that for a time had been a chaise longue dissolved back into the energy that formed it and became part of the Utera once more, part of the featureless, metallic, gray egg.

Athena said, "May I have a chair, please?"

A chair rose from the curved inner surface of the eggshell where she was standing. It scooped her up within itself like a nest. It cushioned her comfortably, and utterly molded itself to her exquisite features. It allowed her to move, to adjust her weight to a new position at will, accommodating her new shape each time she changed position. And it lifted her high above the deck suspended atop a singular, telescoping pole.

Xuxa's three-dimensional mental projection floated up to join her. "Here is what I detected," said Xuxa, as she gracefully gestured once again with her right hand. Before them, the curved inner wall of the dull, gray egg became translucent. And shimmering upon the ephemeral media was the Angel system seen from its outer asteroid belt looking inward toward their frigid destination and its dim, brown binary stars.

Athena reached out with her right hand and touched Xuxa's interior wall with her fingertips ever so lightly. The inside wall of Utera Davidos was covered in sensory cilia, and when Athena touched the hairs ever so lightly, it sent the Utera into a state of such calmness that Xuxa's thoughts drifted and she often fell asleep. Athena was amused that she could make Xuxa sleep with a touch much like turning a small alligator on its back and rubbing its belly, as was once done on ancient Earth.

And when Xuxa dreamed, she would often contemplate where she and her Uteran sisters came from and where they had journeyed to within the Milky Way in search of God. At first, when her ancestors contemplated God, while they swam in a tepid sea upon their home world millions of years ago, they thought that their deity was in the sky. They thought that the sun was God. And the desire to be near their creator was their motivation for evolving mentally, and for journeying into space itself. But once there, they quickly discovered that the sun was not the deity. Even though the sun warmed their planet, light from it acting on chlorophyll turned water and air into sugar, and every creature on their world was literally made of star stuff, it was not God. It was not the conscious extralucent mind that they believed God was, whom they sang to while standing on their heads as male humpback whales once did on moonless nights on ancient Earth. And it was not the mind of fire and light that they heard whispering to them in the deep recesses of their thoughts every night while they slept.

As Xuxa journeyed amid the stars of the Milky Way, slipping from system to system like a water boatman skimming the surface tension between the stars, she looked upward still, but now at the other galaxies within the universe. And she wondered if God was in any of them. She guessed that he was not there either. She speculated that he existed in another dimension, in some place beyond the physical limitations of space, stars, and galaxies, maybe even beyond the universe itself. And she pondered how she and her sisters could make the leap there just as the first Uterans, so long ago, pondered about the sun and thought themselves upward, out of the ocean, through the air, and into space.

Athena laughed. "Xuxa," she called. "Wake up, Xuxa." The behemoth awakened with a shudder. And the mental projection of her, whose head had been resting on Athena's lap, while the Mother Superior caressed her fiery-orange hair, opened its eyes. "There you are," said Athena, who pointed to the transparent wall. "See what I see."

Xuxa sat up. And together they viewed Angel from just outside the system, just before Utera Davidos penetrated the magnetic froth of the heliosheath, echoing with low frequency radio noise, and entered the sluggish solar winds of the outer heliosphere.

The Uteran and the Tellusian looked inside the rocky outer rim of the binary brown dwarf system but could barely see the two suns. From that distance, the stars were a pin prick, at best, and barely visible, so dim that they appeared as one, and so cold that the methane rich suns themselves had water clouds in their atmospheres. The dwarfs were closer to giant exoplanets than stars, a mere fifty times the size of Jupiter in the Sol system, and lacked the mass to initiate nuclear fusion and stellar illumination. Yet, as remarkable as it was, the Angel system contained life. Moreso, it contained intelligent, technological life as defined by the ancient Drake Equation.

The symbiotes looked past the smaller outlying gas giants toward the ringed giant in middle orbit around the binary stars. The slightly flattened helium and hydrogen sphere held within its outer ring a moon the size of Tellus Mater that harbored advanced alien life where no life should have taken hold to start with. The world was called Lesta.

The entire Angel system was outside of the galactic habitable zone, in a harsh part of the Milky Way, where it was exposed to high levels of cosmic radiation. And the moon Lesta itself was outside of the circumstellar habitable zone of the Angel system, caught in the outer ring of a planetary subsystem, in an area of space orbiting the brown dwarfs and again orbiting its primary gas giant where water existed only in a deeply frozen state. Yet, as the flattened, frozen ellipsoid orbited the giant, the pull and push of tidal forces deformed the moon and melted its rocky aluminum and iron core. The molten interior melted a deep layer of water ice far beneath the perpetually frozen exterior. A salt water ocean formed. And within the ocean, life began.

God's experiment in cold life that he threw out into the sands of the multiverse shaped like a starfish on the floor of the Mandala Room of Heaven had taken seed on Lesta, despite the odds, and had flourished beyond all expectation. And over time, a bipedal creature evolved in God's image that resembled the humans of Earth so long ago and so far away. And they were good. And God was pleased.

Lesta appeared to Xuxa and to Athena to be an ice ball covered in craters, depressions, grooves, plains and ridges in its northern hemisphere. Whereas, its southern hemisphere was covered in cryovolcanic vents that spewed blue plumes of hydrocarbons, molecular nitrogen, and salt water high into space. The plumes fed the ring within which the moon orbited. And the less energetic ejecta fell back on the southern hemisphere of Lesta as snow, turning it into the brightest object of its size in the entire Angel system.

The Daughters of Tellus Mater, listening with their radio telescopes, heard the Lestans for a thousand years before the people of the icy moon heard them. What they heard, once their computers scrubbed the Lestan signal from the background electronic hiss of the cosmos, was an intelligent signal, even in its raw state. It was not the rapid, staccato, chewing gum card against bicycle spokes flapping of spinning pulsars. It was not the high pitched whine of gas giants nor was it the crackle of sunspots from yellow stars on the main sequence. What they heard was organized. And when they analyzed it, they were overjoyed because the signal was not merely digital containing a plethora of information about the Lestans. It was creative. It was musical. And what they heard was singing. It came from the system that the natives called Angel. And it came from a people that called the moon they inhabited Lesta.

The singing came from the largest church on the icy moon. The place of worship emerged from the Great Lestan Sea like upturned icicles resembling a hand reaching upward to touch God. But it was not made from the ice that covered their world. It was made from the sugar sand that surrounded their subglacial sea and the germanium created long ago by the slow capture of lighter elements inside a pulsating red giant star found now mixed with copper, lead, and zinc. The Lestans fused the silica and the germanium and manufactured five thousand rectangular panes of glass. They affixed the panes to a fragile frame of aluminum over a period of twenty years. And when all was said and done, they completed an architectural wonder and a thing of beauty.

They called their creation the Ice Cathedral. It was functional. It was a church. It was a place of comfort and congregation. But it was more than that. It was also a gigantic radio transmitter. From the icicles, from the fingers, from the pointy pinnacles of the prayer spires amplified radio transmissions emerged, penetrated the icy roof of the ice cavern in which they lived, and pulsed into space. And it was those transmissions from the cathedral's pointy peeks that the Tellusians heard when they listened with their radio telescopes.

Utera Davidos approached Lesta as the icy moon entered the shadow of the gas giant. A xenon flash pulsed amid the darkness on the backside of the moon to indicate the landing site. As the living starship closed on the location in the pockmarked northern hemisphere, four xenon lights flashing in unison could be discerned. Pairs of lights were positioned equidistant from each other on two sides of a substantial crack in the icy lunar cover. The crack was a giant crevasse five hundred miles long, ten miles across, and five miles deep that tapered from top to bottom like a wedge.

Xuxa descended past the pulsing xenon lights into the pitch black crevasse. Far beneath her was a white light surrounded by red lights. As she navigated downward, pairs of red lights positioned on either side of the crevasse ascended. Red lights within red lights passed the descending ship until only the white light remained below. The white light became four passive lights. The living egg slowed its descent. And it landed softly on the prescribed pad, at the bottom of the crevasse, within a gigantic ice cave that contained a breathable atmosphere, upon an island of solid ground surrounded by a subterranean salt water sea.

And Xuxa was overjoyed because it reminded her of home.

Chapter 4 - portent

The arrival of Utera Davidos on planet Lesta was met with great fanfare. The inhabitants of the planet had heard about the Tellusians for a very long time. The Tellusians were discussed by the highest government officials around the world, and around the supper tables of the planet's humblest citizens. The Daughters of Tellus Mater had been talked about, debated over, and written about since first contact was made over radio a thousand years before. They had been expected for so long that they had become the stuff of legend. Bit by bit, an exchange of knowledge, philosophy, and science had taken place over the millennia. And now, at long last, the Tellusians were there. They had made the long journey across the stars, across space and time from the Sol system to the Angel system, and had finally arrived at Lesta.

Magazines had written about the Tellusians extensively in the past year, as Utera Davidos began to brake from near light speed, and the arrival neared. Newspapers published a daily countdown. Students were given the day off school to attend the welcome ceremony. And the area around the landing pad, built to Tellusian specifications, was packed shoulder to shoulder with ten thousand students.

The Lestans cooed as Utera Davidos entered the atmosphere and navigated toward touchdown before them. Presidents of countries around the planet gasped as the spaceship descended. Dignitaries straightened their ties. The organic spaceship was far beyond anything they had ever imagined or constructed. The technology was thousands of years in advance of their crude machines. They watched in amazement as Utera Davidos descended silently, shed frosted Angel hair from its cool exterior, and landed like a feather on the designated landing pad.

Tellusian Seed by Mark Carter

There was no heat from the spacecraft. There was no radiation. There was no release of noxious gas. There was only a song that some Lestans said they heard as the starship entered the atmosphere. But once the ship was at rest all that could be discerned was the evaporation of a thin coating of ice from the hull of the spaceship.

The crowd held their breaths as Lestan technicians in bright yellow, rubberized, radiation suits walked around the ship and took readings that all read in the clear. Technicians in green coveralls took samples of the Angel hair that fell upon the crowd, the ice that quickly evaporated from the hull, and the gas that surrounded the ship. But they found nothing out of the ordinary either. The technicians gave the expectant officials the thumbs up. And the crowd cheered.

A brass band started to play the Tellusian anthem to welcome their guests. And everyone stood out of respect.

Shortly after, a small crack in the shape of a portal appeared on the side of the Utera where no crack was discerned before. A door slid upward. The first Tellusian that the Lestans had ever seen live appeared in the doorway. And a gasp swept through the crowd.

Everyone knew what the Tellusians looked like. They had provided pictures of themselves to the Lestans for hundreds of years. But the photographs did not do them justice. It was only after seeing them live, as the Tellusian missionaries to a strange world debarked from Utera Davidos, that the hair-matted, pock-marked, scabbed and scarred Lestans realized how utterly beautiful the alabaster-skinned Tellusians were, despite the fact that they were nuns.

When the Gabrielican Sisters of Atonement appeared, Lestan clairvoyants sensed that something was amiss. They sensed it the moment that a portal opened in Utera Davidos and the long expected alien missionaries debarked. The clairvoyants weren't sure what or when. When asked, all they would say is, "Soon." They were told by officials that they were merely picking up sensations of the long expected Tellusian landing. But the clairvoyants shook their heads, and said, "No." When they were asked what was going to happen, they were vague because that is the nature of extrasensory perception. When asked if it was a disaster that they sensed, they got very serious, and said, "Yes," then shook their heads and added, "and no." Their enigmatic answer confused everyone. "Which is it?" yelled a Lestan General who expected a definitive, black and white answer when he asked a question, and not wishy-washy shades of gray. But the clairvoyants merely smiled, and said, "Both. It will be both. It will be something utterly horrifying and absolutely wonderful."

Benefit versus cost. It was what it all came down to with the Lestans, as it usually does with most people, companies, countries, and worlds who want to advance quickly and are willing to do whatever it takes. And with the government of Lesta, particularly the military, the benefit of communication and visitation by the Tellusians, with the potential of technological sharing or stealing, made the cost of chronic exposure to germanium acceptable.

Whereas the crowd, eyes irritated, skin blistered, and lungs and throats burned by chronic exposure to germanium chloride in their sub-glacial atmosphere, was mesmerized by the charismatic nuns with their alabaster skin, the gas-masked Lestan military was interested in the organic starship. And shortly after the Tellusians debarked, while they were busied with the trappings of brass bands, speeches, and other honors foisted upon them during the welcoming ceremonies by Lestan officials crippled with renal dysfunction, hepatic stenosis, and peripheral neuropathy, military technicians crawled over Utera Davidos like brown ants on an earthworm.

When the curtain of Lestan deceit was pulled back, the real reason behind their acceptance of the Tellusian proposal to send missionaries to their world to share the *Book of Gabriel* and the Word of the Mother was revealed. For years, the Lestan military had planned to dissect the living Uteran technology, and to reverse engineer it for their own purposes. It was as devious and as simple as that. The Tellusians had been duped. The eventful day had arrived. The time was now. And the Lestan military jumped at the opportunity.

Chapter 5 - monsters

While the Gabrielican Sisters of Atonement were in conference, Xuxa slept, to conserve energy, atop the landing pad at the bottom of the Great Crevasse beneath the icy exterior of Lesta. She was destined to live off of her fat stores for the duration of their time there, since the dim, binary stars of the Angel system provided her with no sustenance. But it was during her deep repose that Lestan military technicians mounted the landing pad with their Head Spades, Boarding Knives, Blubber Pikes, and Gaffs to commence the flensing of the whale.

The Lestans, in general, saw little difference between Utera Davidos and the behemoths that swam the depths of the Great Lestan Sea whom they harpooned, and whose exterior they flensed into large sheets of blubber, and boiled down for oil. If it wasn't for the military who desired to dissect the Utera themselves and reverse engineer her organic technology, the whaling conglomerate would have made fast work of her where she was. To them, she looked and smelled like a cooked beef roast sitting upon a cutting board waiting to be sliced.

Xuxa had been staring at the vast, subsurface, lunar sea since making her landing there. And when she fell asleep, she dreamed of her home world so far away and long ago. Although she had been born in space to creatures who once lived in the ocean but thought themselves into space, and who now lived permanently between the stars, the sight of the Great Lestan Sea, and the smell of salt water awoke genetic memories hard wired at the molecular level within her. And she suddenly wanted nothing more than to return to the waters from which her kind once thrived.

The genetic memory of how to feed, to mate, and to nurture her young in the tepid, tropical waters of her home world, stored in the code of purines and pyrimidines supporting her ascending and descending chains of ribose sugar within the nuclear chromosomes of every cell in her body, tugged at her. Until she landed on Lesta, she had not been aware of the terrible longing she possessed, that all of her evolved kind had, to return to their home world, every generation, and to the sea. It was a longing deeper than any hunger. It was a longing shared by the salmon of ancient Earth that pushed them from the ocean on the seventh year of their lives to seek the fresh water rivers and upland streams of their origin, to turn scarlet and deformed with hormones, to procreate, and to die. It was a million year desire stored in Xuxa's DNA. And the sight and smell of the Sea awoke it within her.

Xuxa slept so soundly that she was oblivious to the first few yard-wide chunks of her exterior, as they were sliced from her. But her biotechnology was more sensitive the deeper the technicians cut and probed. And finally, she awoke in panic, and sensing a threat to her well-being, she did what comes naturally to Utera. She returned to the sea.

Her first instinct was to flee. When her ancestors lived in the sea, they released a squirt of black ink, and jetted away during the momentary confusion. So, in a carryover of her lineage, Xuxa defensively, instinctively, and reflexively released black smoke to facilitate her escape. And she flew away, dragging electrical cables, cutting torches, ventilation ductwork, and Lestan technicians behind her as she leaped into the air of the ice cave and headed out over the Great Lestan Sea.

The Lestan military commanders had foreseen her attempt to escape and had equipment standing by to ensnare her. And so, when Xuxa leaped into the air of the ice cave and flew out over the Great Lestan Sea, the military fired upon the whale-like behemoth that she was with harpoons.

Xuxa flew out over the aquamarine shallows to where the bottom dropped off and the water turned cobalt blue, cold, and dark. She soared down, landed on the surface, and submerged herself. She would be safe there.

And it was glorious, like steeping in a hot bath after freezing in the deep cold of space.

The dark, deep ocean was where she belonged. She knew it instinctively. It was where food would be plentiful. And it was. She thought herself a mouth with baleen brush and tongue, a stomach, and intestines, and metamorphosed into a creature resembling a Humpback whale of ancient Earth. And as she swam she caught tons of crustaceans resembling shrimp in her filter, tongued them down her gullet, and rolled back her eyes in ecstasy. In all the time she had lived in space and fed off of the gamma rays emitted by suns, she had never known such intoxication. And she wanted more. She desired the aroma, the flavor, and the texture of food. She desired the sensual feeling of cool water passing over her external hairs. She desired the echolocation images of her pitch black surroundings in flashes of white against cobalt blue.

For the time being, she had escaped the danger posed by the Lestan technicians. But the damage they did to her body leaked a trail of blood and plasma into the unfamiliar waters, and would bring another type of danger to her.

Xuxa broadcast her revelry to the stars, at the speed of thought, to her sisters spread across the galaxy. They heard her. And they sent back their messages of dread. "Daisy," they called across the galactic expanse, "Daisy. You are in danger."

"That is nonsense," she replied. "I was in danger, but now I am sublime."

"Daisy," they cried amid the stars, utterly distressed by her exuberance. "Look around you for we can see what you ignore."

"I am in no danger," said Xuxa. "What you see are large schools of small creatures. What you see is food, and the eating of it in the old way of our ancestors. And it is glorious."

"We cry for you," they called to her across billions of stars. "We cry for you, sister, because you are blind, and we have already lost you."

Xuxa thought about their words and assumed that they meant she had devolved and would not return to her evolved state. She assumed they meant that she was so enticed by sensation that she would be unable to give it up. But now that she had experienced it, she was sure she would be able to return. She knew now that she would be satisfied, and that satisfaction would last for a very long time.

It hit her like a cut, then a pierce, then so many stabs that she became disoriented. She had never had a sensation like it before and didn't know what to do. She experienced pain. She had lancinating pain everywhere.

Tellusian Seed by Mark Carter

Hidden within the schools of shrimp-like creatures were packs of shark-like predators called *lamia* who hunted the Great Lestan Sea like packs of wolves for large creatures like herself. If Xuxa had bothered to ask any Lestan, they would have told her that it was dangerous to journey into the dark depths. They would have told her: *there be monsters there.* They would have warned her of the danger. But, despite her age, she was inexperienced in such things. She was not always a good communicator. And she was impetuous.

A crowd collected on the shore of the Sea near the landing pad that Xuxa had abandoned. And the news spread quickly, even into the conference itself, about the attack on the Uteran ship by military technicians, and about the drama being played out a mile off shore. Athena was alarmed when she was told of the evolving situation and came running outside to see for herself. But it was already too late.

What Athena witnessed was the beginning of the end. She covered her mouth with her hands to stifle her scream of horror because what she saw offshore was the brutal slaying of a sentient but foolish creature by voracious alien sharks. Every bite of Xuxa's flesh elicited fountains of blood which could be seen from a mile away. There was blood everywhere. Athena had never seen so much blood. The ocean in that spot became blood.

Athena looked away because her heart was broken and she could take no more of the gruesome display. She paused for a moment, closed her eyes, and composed herself. It was only then that the gravity of the situation hit her.

If circumstances changed for the worst with the Lestans, there was now no means of escape. With Xuxa gone, they were marooned there. The Utera, through the disingenuous actions of the Lestan military, and through her own exuberance and naivety, had become the first casualty of the grand Tellusian mission to seed the stars of the Milky Way with the Word of God.

A crowd of horror struck Lestan and Tellusian onlookers stood on the shore of the Great Lestan Sea with hands over mouths shocked by the carnage they had just witnessed. And when the fountain of blood subsided, and the struggle was over, and the flesh of the Utera was ripped to pieces, waves generated by the altercation crashed at their feet, first clear and frothy with salt, then red and frothy with blood. And so, the life that evolved from an ocean and carried a miniature ocean within itself, was poured back into the great bowl, and became one again. And the Lestans and the Tellusians wept because it was all so sad.

What infuriated Athena about the incident was that Xuxa was devoured by clearly inferior creatures. Yet it happened all of the time on Tellus Mater and elsewhere every minute of every day to those who didn't use their evolved brains to avoid danger. Xuxa clearly had not used hers. Her evolved telekinetic abilities had allowed her species to travel into space with a thought, and to navigate the stars. But her base instincts, the hard-wired sensual and sexual circuits of an older brain sealed within the wrapper of the new had caused Xuxa to succumb to desires that put her in jeopardy. She had acted stupidly. And for a few moments of revelry, she had paid the ultimate price. It was such a waste.

Even Athena, despite advanced evolutionary status, education, and experience, did not fully comprehend what she had just seen. Her emotions got in the way. She only saw an ending, and was angered by what she saw. But energy can neither be created nor destroyed. It can only be transformed from one state to another. Nothing is ever wasted. Dead stars themselves are recycled and live on in us. And Utera Davidos possessed more energy than Athena realized.

And so, from the bloody froth that washed ashore, like Aphrodite rising from the spent sperm of Kronos, Xuxa arose naked with fiery-orange hair from the foam of the Great Lestan Sea, and came to shore on the half-shell like her Roman counterpart from ancient Earth mythology. Only now, she was no longer the mental projection of Utera Davidos as Athena last saw her. She was Xuxa in and of herself. She looked Tellusian because it was a physical form that she considered beautiful. But she was now other and moreso than the Gabrielican Sisters of Atonement. She had metamorphosed. In the midst of adversity, she had evolved inadvertently to the next level on her quest to find God.

The charismatic power of Xuxa, the literal waves of light emanating from her, bent onlookers at the knee. Even Mother Superior herself and her cloister of Gabrielican nuns got down upon their knees. And like the others in the crowd, Athena wept. She couldn't help herself. It was the effect that Xuxa had on her now. The hearts and souls of the Lestans and the Tellusians alike were filled with joy from being in the radiant presence of an Angel. And in far off star systems throughout the galaxy, her Uteran sisters wept too.

The first Lestans to witness the angelic presence of Xuxa stood in place for days, in the way they calculate days, and even died in place for lack of food and water, mesmerized by the perceived deific creature that appeared in their midst. The hapless victims of the evolved Uteran presence had to be escorted to hospital for help. But they were ever after altered by the experience. They spoke of, "the light," and about, "understanding it all now." But when asked what they understood they could not explain. It was as if they were sleepwalking, caught in a dream from which they could not awaken.

They repeated the word, "Angel." Some said, "I see Angels everywhere."

In Lestan religious mythology, the term Angels meant creatures from the afterlife. And the reason they stood in place when they saw Xuxa arise from the bloody foam on the shore of the Great Lestan Sea was that they expected to die right there and then and be taken away to the Lestan concept of Heaven by the Angel that appeared before them.

Chapter 6 - angel

The physical metamorphosis and ethereal transmigration of Xuxa from Uteran to Tellusian was a miracle to the Lestans and to the Gabrielican Sisters of Atonement alike, but it turned the intended mission of the nuns on its ear. In and of itself, the transformation was proof that Angels exist, and indirectly that God exists. And that was good for the missionaries because many Lestans, just as the people of the old Earth before Lucifer's devastating impact, had come to doubt the existence of God in his Heaven. Her transformation helped to convince them that the messages in the *Book of Gabriel* had validity. But it was also bad because Xuxa had no intention of remaining on the icy moon. And she wanted Mother Superior to come with her.

After searching for God all of her life, Xuxa suddenly sensed where he could be found. Moreover, she now had the means to complete the last leg of her journey. She desired to take the Tellusians with her because she cared about them. They were kindred spirits. And she loved them dearly. She always had. It was her hope and prayer that they would ascend soon too, by whatever means. And if she could help, she would. So, she didn't want them out of her sight.

Xuxa stood naked on the shoreline of the Sea, and faced a crowd of shocked onlookers who had just witnessed the bloody evisceration of Utera Davidos and her miraculous rebirth as an Angel. And in the midst of that surreal moment, she stopped to marvel at the beauty of fingers. She never imagined, even though she had taken the projected form of a Tellusian and knew what fingers were, that she would ever actually possess fingers herself. Yet, there she was with fingers and toes, a stunningly beautiful body, fiery-orange hair, and diaphanous wings. It was physicality in ethereal form. And she was pleased.

She sensed amazement coming from the crowd, some sexual arousal, and some fear. And she accepted it as what it was considering the situation and her lack of attire. So she imagined a double-girded chiton of ancient Greek design, and clothed herself in it. On her feet she imagined leather sandals. And it was so.

Down the beach to her left there stood a small group of high ranking Lestan military officers who projected only hatred toward Xuxa because she had ruined their plans to reverse engineer Utera Davidos. To them, the alien spacecraft was organic technology, and nothing more. It was not a living, sensitive, sentient creature. And they had intended to eviscerate the alien craft while the Tellusians were distracted in their conference with Lestan and other alien dignitaries. They had intended to chop up the starship while it rested on the landing pad, transport it elsewhere, and analyze it for years, if need be to discover its technological secrets.

"Athena?" thought Xuxa.

"I hear you," thought Athena, as she struggled to work her way through the tight crowd. "How are you, my darling? What are you? How is any of this possible? You should be dead."

"Yes," thought Xuxa. "And I thought I was dead. Instead, through some mechanism that I do not comprehend, I have become. I have shed my body and am entirely spirit now. And as such, my voice is meant for the ears of God. Tell these devout people here to cover their ears for the Angel is about to speak, but not to them. Tell them that they will perish if they hear my full voice." Athena warned the people. They covered their ears. Then Xuxa proceeded.

The Angel turned toward the military officers and spoke in a voice that sounded like a thousand brass horns. The power of it terrified the onlookers. But it blew the officers off their feet to grovel on the sand. She did not do it to force them to respect her. That was pointless. She did it to attract their attention and in no uncertain terms to make them know that she had read their minds and knew about their plan to eviscerate Utera Davidos. Moreover, she knew about their standing plan to chop up any Utera that ever landed there again. She wanted them to know that there would be severe consequences.

Had Xuxa been so inclined, she could have squashed them like sow bugs with the slightest effort of mind for their attempt at her life. But she had no animosity. She possessed no hatred. As a species, the Uterans were benevolent. And as an Angel, Xuxa was benevolence personified. But when it came to her family and friends, to her sister Utera and the Gabrielican nuns, she was protective and would do just about anything to ensure their wellbeing including destroying a world with a thought, if need be.

Xuxa's message to the military officers was clear. "Mark what I say," she thundered, "for my word is absolute and my powers are vast. Others of my kind know what has transpired here today. And they shall be coming. If any harm befalls my sister Utera when they come to transform, or if any harm befalls the lamia in the Great Lestan Sea destined to eviscerate them and therefore prevents the transformation of my sisters, I shall wreak vengeance upon you. Do not test my patience. It is but a simple matter for me to crush your miniscule and icy moon with a passing thought."

Xuxa turned her attention back to the onlookers kneeling in fear and respect before her, and her heart went out to them. This was never what she expected or wanted. And she wished that they would all merely get up.

When the Lestans looked upon her, they saw a winged Angel from their mythology, someone who looked like a transcended version of themselves. When dignitaries from other worlds, who were also in attendance, looked upon Xuxa, they too saw a creature from their own religious lore.

But when Athena broke through the crowd and looked upon Xuxa, at the mental projection of the slain Utera made manifest, she saw something wonderful. Beyond the fact that Xuxa was more than Utera now and had truly evolved to the next level was the simple fact that Xuxa was alive. And to Athena, who had been Xuxa's dearest friend for years, it was the most important thing of all.

Athena saw that Xuxa had taken the Tellusian form as her own, but was essentially non-corporeal and formless. Unlike her Tellusian friends who were more ethereal than corporeal, adversity had driven Utera Davidos to metamorphose beyond that state, to skip a step, and to become utterly ethereal. As such, she could travel anywhere in the universe, and maybe even beyond, with a thought. She could be in multiple places at once. And she could see beyond.

Xuxa understood now that there were eight universes, a literal multiverse shaped like a starfish on the floor of something called the Mandala Room of Heaven in the place that she and her sister Utera had searched for all of their lives. She knew where Heaven was now. And with the power of mind, she now had the means to get there. She also knew that a similar destiny but different path was in store for her Tellusian friends.

"Are you just going to stand there?" thought the Angel to her friend.

Athena ran into Xuxa's waiting arms and melted into her embrace.

"I thought I had lost you," thought the Tellusian.

"Never," thought Xuxa. "Have you seen what I have seen?"

"Yes," thought Athena.

"Then you know what I must do," thought Xuxa.

"Just go," thought Athena. "No long good-byes."

"I am not going alone, my friend," thought Xuxa. "I have seen my future, and yours. And they exist in separate realms. But my part in the here and now is to deliver you and two others to where you must be to fulfill your destiny. You have no future here. You will think me a fool, at first blush, to bring you where I must. But time will prove the wisdom of my ways. My destiny lies elsewhere also, but not with you. But be not dismayed for our paths shall cross again. Of that you can be certain, for I have seen it."

"Oh, Xuxa," thought Athena, while she sobbed, "you are too kind."

"Would you not do the same for me, if you stood where I stand?" thought Xuxa.

"Without question," thought Athena.

"Then put an end to your tears," thought Xuxa, "for I need your help. You must intercede on my behalf before these Lestan dignitaries and onlookers. You must be my voice."

Athena nodded, wiped her cheeks, and said, "I understand."

"The nun talks with the Angel,' said a Lestan in the crowd, who witnessed Athena nodding, crying, and speaking.

"What does she say?" asked another Lestan onlooker.

"The Tellusian says she understands."

Athena turned and faced the crowd. And standing shoulder to shoulder with the Angel, she said, "I am Athena. You have all seen me and have heard me speak since my sisters and I arrived. You know me to speak the truth. The Angel has asked me to speak to you for her."

"Let the Angel speak again," yelled an idiot at the back of the crowd.

"How do we know that you're telling us what it says?" shouted a second disruptor.

"How is it that it speaks only to you?" heckled a third.

"The Angel speaks to my mind," said Athena. "And I speak back to her, in kind, for she is a creature of energy, light, and spirit. Because of the vast difference between you and her, there is a communication abyss. So, she has asked me to bridge the gap. And I do this service gladly."

"Liar," yelled an atheist and cynic before being muzzled and removed by security.

Athena's Tellusian sisters, who had been working their way through the crowd, as well, joined her and Xuxa, and stood shoulder to shoulder with them in solidarity.

"I hear her also," said the first Gabrielican nun.

"As do I," said the second nun.

"And I," said the third.

And the heckling stopped.

"I know," said Athena, "that this turn of events is unexpected. It wasn't on the itinerary. We Gabrielican Sisters of Atonement, we missionary nuns, were invited here to teach you the Word of the Mother. And, to that end, we have journeyed a great distance to be your mentors. But this event, this miracle, has changed all of that. No sooner have we arrived than some of us must depart. And for that, I apologize. Soon, this Angel will be leaving, and she is taking three of us with her, including myself, because our destinies lie elsewhere. Seven sisters will stay behind to teach you our ways."

"Take us too," yelled a hooligan.

"We want to go."

Athena held up the palm of her right hand and the crowd quieted.

"But first," said Athena, "the Angel bids that I speak her words." Xuxa looked at Athena, and thought her thoughts, which Athena, in turn, spoke to the onlookers. "When God," said Athena, "threw his seed out into the void, he never expected life to take hold on Lesta. Yet here you are. You are a miracle. You have survived and even flourished. And for that, God is pleased. I ask you to believe in God for he exists in all things. And I ask you to believe in yourselves for you are special and precious in his eyes."

The Gabrielican paused and looked at the Angel one again. Xuxa touched Athena with her thoughts. And the Gabrielican continued. "The Angel Xuxa bids me to tell you," she said, "that she sees what has made you ill, and shall cleanse your world of it. She also gives me this message: Wash in the Great Lestan Sea, and you shall be healed. This miracle she performs in the name of God."

"God be praised," cried a Lestan.

"And lastly," said Athena, "the Angel Xuxa says: be good to one another. And so saying, we bid you farewell."

Athena gathered her Gabrielican sisters around her in a tight huddle, and spoke quietly with them. She explained to them how and why she chose the youngest and the most inexperienced among them to accompany the Angel and herself. And the others could see the wisdom of her ways. Good-byes were said. Tears were spent. Breasts were pulled to breasts. Cheeks were kissed. Good luck was exchanged. And lastly, she reminded those who were to remain that they still had a mission. And they all laughed.

And when everything was said and done, the Angel Xuxa wrapped her wings around the chosen Daughters and vanished, leaving the seven sisters, dignitaries, and onlookers in surreal shock, wondering if any of what they had just witnessed had ever occurred. Then, one by one, the diseased Lestans made their way to the sea, submerged themselves, and were healed, as Athena said, by the grace of God through the intervention and kindness of a nascent Messenger.

Chapter 7 - temptation

S oon after Xuxa departed Lesta with the three Gabrielicans, her
sister Utera began to arrive on the icy moon. One by one, they
submerged themselves in the dark water of the Great Lestan Sea,
as she had. And, like her, they were viciously attacked, stripped, and
killed by Lamia. The horror and the pain metamorphosed them. And
they arose, like Xuxa, from the bloody froth of their own brutal demise
as naked Angels with beautiful bodies, fiery-orange hair, and
diaphanous wings.

With their new perceptions, the nascent Messengers saw where
Heaven was. They realized that it was finally within their grasp. And,
with a thought, they clothed themselves and journeyed out of the Milky
Way, beyond the seventh universe, and across the cobalt blue Celestial
Sea to Paradise.

Despite Xuxa's warning that she would crush their world with a
thought if the military interfered with the metamorphosis of the Uterans
to Angels, the Lestan Generals could not help themselves. They
desperately wanted to reverse engineer the living starships. And they
could only stand by for so long and watch the advanced technology slip
through their fingers and purposefully succumb to the voracious alien
sharks before they acted to achieve their goals. The military waited and
watched for the right opportunity. And during a lull in the Uteran
arrivals and transformations, when only one behemoth was on the icy
moon, they pounced. And the Utera was theirs.

They attacked the behemoth called Sasha as she arrived at the
bottom of the ice cave from her chilly journey across space and time.
They attacked her before she oriented herself, before she acclimatized
to the heat of the chamber and the low light level. They attacked her

with the only thing that could subdue her. They hit her with high frequency sound.

Like the behemoths of the old Earth who plied the seas before Lucifer's devastation, and who were driven insane by submarine sonar, and beached themselves, Sasha was struck by the Lestan high frequency emission and fell unconscious. But before she succumbed to the dizzy and frightening sensation of losing control and falling, she screamed her fear into the void. And she was heard by every Utera in the galaxy. She was even heard by Xuxa, in Heaven, in another dimension entirely, and so very far away.

Then Sasha sank from the high air in the ice cave, as Utera do when they sleep or are unconscious, and came to rest on her side upon the broad sand beach of the Great Lestan Sea. And Lestans whalers were all over her.

The Captain and the first mate of the whaling ship White Lamia, in the employ of the military, attacked her and made fast work of her. With deft strokes of Head Spades and Boarding Knives, they flensed a spiral of flesh around the behemoth from head to tail. Then, with Blubber Pikes, Gaffs, pulleys and ropes, they pulled away her flesh in one, continuous, bloody blanket.

If Sasha had been a Lestan whale, the blanket would have been sliced into sections, thrown into a large cooking pot, and boiled down for oil. But the military had another agenda. And the blanket was sliced into sections and shipped to various labs for analysis of its metallurgy, radiation absorbance and resistance, stealthiness, and strength, in the hope of reverse engineering the material. And Sasha's interior was sliced into bits and pieces too and shipped off to military labs interested in what allowed the living ship to alter its features without hydraulics, communicate without electronics, and to fly from star to star at the speed of light without engines or apparent fuel.

The military had what it needed but was greedy for another Utera. Why reverse engineer one beast when you could examine a dozen or more? And the whalers were happy too. They had been allowed to keep a relic of the alien vivisection as a souvenir of their catch: a flexible titanium pump the size of a large turkey from Earth of long ago resembling a massive heart. And as they slipped and slid hip deep in Uteran blood while carrying the object away, the Captain and first mate boasted about the season's worth of blood-stained cash they had earned courtesy of one catch. And they dreamed about the cornucopia of profit that was to come.

Xuxa sought out the Mother of Creation in the Rose Garden of Heaven and begged her for guidance concerning the matter on Lesta. And Diana was compassionate and patient. She asked the young Angel to sit on a marble bench. And she sat down beside her. Then God told her about creation and destruction, and why both were necessary. She spoke about duty, honor, and responsibility. She spoke about *noblesse oblige*, pain, and sacrifice. She spoke about the War of Heaven, Lucifera's corruption, the death of Hephzibah and Adonai and the sacrifice they all made to reunite the lovers. She spoke about the crucifixion, and the necessity of it.

"Being an Angel is not as easy as corporeal creatures imagine," said the Mother. "It is not about dancing, harp playing, and lounging upon clouds. It is about breaking a sweat in the wheat fields of Heaven. It is about being a Messenger for Father, Son, and me to the most desolate places in the multiverse. It is about representing us and our wishes throughout reality. It is about acknowledging and sometimes rewarding goodness. And it is about punishing evil, although, in many places, it is long overdue. And when our will is disobeyed, as it has been on Lesta, it is about administering the Hand of God. But it is also about patience and time to let destiny run its course as written by God Almighty in his *Great Book*."

"I am unsure," said Xuxa, "how much punishment to administer to the Lestans."

The Mother of Creation looked into Xuxa's mind and saw that the neophyte Angel's initial emotional reaction to the death of her sister Utera at the hands of the Lestans was to annihilate their icy world. She wanted to fly free, to let loose, and to blast the rocky snowball and everyone within it to shards destined to orbit the gas giant as a ring of particulates. But she didn't rush to administer her severe vengeance. She had doubts. So, she asked for advice. And God was pleased with Xuxa's temperance.

"We are creatures," said the Mother of Creation, "of great passion and of equally great power. By not reacting immediately, as your passion dictated, you have already proven your metal, my young Angel. Such wisdom in one so young is rare indeed and shall serve you well. Many of my own Angels have not been so wise, and have done despicable things. Some have annihilated worlds, as was your first inclination. Others have destroyed systems. A few have decimated galaxies. One wiped out an entire universe, but that was long ago. My advice to you concerning Lesta is to look into the future of the people of that world. Then decide what you wish to do. I have already peered into your future, dearest Xuxa, and shall miss you for it is your destiny to serve another god in her Haven who is not yet but soon shall be."

Diana and Xuxa talked in the Rose Garden for three days. Then Xuxa thanked the Mother, kissed the right hand of God, and departed Heaven to carry out her arduous task.

Xuxa and ninety-nine of her transformed sisters, dressed in golden armor over white tunics with high gold crowns atop heads of fiery-orange hair and with golden sandals upon their feet, journeyed from Heaven, back across the cobalt blue Celestial Sea, and through the seventh universe to the Angel system, to a gas giant, and its icy moon. They came as thieves in the night while the Lestans slept. They came not to save Sasha from vivisection at the hands of Lestan biologists, engineers, and whalers working on behalf of the military. What was done was done. Sasha was dead. And her soul was lost forever and scattered. They would mourn for her later. They came because now was the time for vengeance.

The Angels stood shoulder to shoulder and wing to wing in a large circle on the broad beach of the Great Lestan Sea. They extended their right arms, raised their fingertips, and exposed the seal of God Almighty emblazoned on their palms. And they appeared to onlookers as a wheel of fire and light. It was their desire to place the Lestan criminals at the hub of the wheel, and to spew lightning upon them from one hundred rarefied spokes. But it was not their destiny.

"Hold," said Xuxa to her sister avenging Angels, "and see what I see." So saying, Xuxa and her sisters looked into the future of the Lestans. And they saw Angels there. They noted the blood lines leading to the transcendence of the ice world people and understood that if they killed the perpetrators responsible for Sasha's death, the metamorphosis would never occur. And the Angels bled with deific stigmata, in frustration, because the right thing to do to avenge Sasha's death was to do nothing.

And the Angels shrieked Gabriel's octaval mantra until the frozen ceiling above them hummed and the ice cave threatened to collapse.

Just BEEE.

To protect other arriving Utera from the insatiable technological appetites of the Lestan military, Xuxa assigned twelve Angels to the icy moon. They would see to it that nothing befell the living starships while they metamorphosed into Angels. The remaining Angels were sent back to Heaven to await the birth of a new god who would arise from the rubble of a destroyed civilization.

To prevent the Lestans from reverse engineering a perverse form of Sasha from the bits and pieces of her that they sent to various labs for analysis, the Angels disintegrated every part of their friend. They destroyed the memory of her in the minds of the Lestan military and the biologists, engineers, and whalers that served them. And they destroyed information about the living starships stored on all media. And that was that.

Gradually, an entire race of sensitive and sentient creatures scattered across the Milky Way journeyed to Lesta, sacrificed their behemoth bodies, metamorphosed, and thought themselves to Heaven. After originating in the mind of God Almighty, seeded as cold life, evolving as cuttlefish in a tepid sea, and thinking themselves into the cold radiation of space to lens between the stars, the Uterans instinctively returned home. Like salmon on the old Earth, they returned to their place of origin. They returned to Heaven and to the embrace of their creator.

In returning to God in Heaven, the Uterans instinctively fulfilled what they thought was their destiny. But it was merely the second phase of a longer journey that would take them back to Tellus Mater to serve a new god forged from adversity, like them, but of another kind; and, to work with old symbiotic friends transformed to Angels, in a new Haven, as foretold by the Mother.

Chapter 8 - blame

Future historians from Mars would write in obscure annals that the Tellusian mission to seed the Milky Way with the Word of the Mother through the *Book of Gabriel* was a fool's errand. They would argue that the Tellusians were impetuous and naïve and their carelessness led to the Rancorian attack. Their biased interpretation would deflect the failure of the Martian fleet to protect the Daughters, and instead would plant the blame squarely upon the Daughters themselves for initiating, continuing, and following through with their search for extraterrestrial intelligence. But their accusations and skewed analyses couldn't be further from the truth. They would not take into account the necessity of the attack for Ariel to become god or for Tellus Mater to become the center of the seventh universe for all time.

The Daughters of Tellus Mater sent radio signals into space for a thousand years before they received a return signal. When they finally did, they mulled over the alien response and assigned linguists to learn the alien language, anthropologists to study the alien culture, and psychologists to interpret the alien intentions. They did this for centuries before any decision was ever made to send missionaries out into the galaxy to that alien world. In many cases of alien contact, missionaries were never sent. The aliens were too different physically. Philosophies were incompatible. Their worlds were too hostile.

But most alien contact was positive. In fact, the aliens actually expressed deep emotions and gratitude when they were first contacted. Like creatures stumbling their way through the darkness for so long, the contact with the Tellusians made them feel that they were no longer alone among the stars of the night sky. It was a sentiment that the Tellusians shared.

The decision to select planets was a painstaking process decided by committee after studying the facts, recommendations, and research. There was a call for suggestions about how many ambassadors or missionaries should be sent to each world. And when all was said and done, after academic, political, and scientific considerations, the choice came down to the Gabrielican Sisters of Atonement. They were one of several religious groups on Tellus Mater who embraced the *Book of Gabriel*. But they stood apart because they had been training their disciples for centuries to journey to the stars to spread the Word of the Mother. All of them knew that it would be a one way trip. They knew that it was dangerous. They knew that they might die, and probably would, in the venture. Yet, they volunteered for the privilege of serving the Mother, their order, and Tellus Mater. Moreover, the Gabrielicans were all trained in xenoanthropology, xenolinguistics, and xenopsychology.

Gabrielicans were pulled from nunneries around the world to fill the quota of ten passengers per living starship when the thousand Uteras were launched into the Milky Way on that cool, spring morning. The missionaries were all between sixteen and twenty-eight. They were each implanted with an embryo a month before launch. And they were enthusiastic about their adventure.

For most Gabrielican missionaries, the work they did on their assigned alien worlds went better than expected. For some, it was less than hoped. For others, it was a disaster. But for those who traveled to Alterna, their mission went sideways, and what was expected to be a dream from Heaven became a nightmare from Hell.

Chapter 9 - gallus

When the Tellusians viewed the Alternans, as they had on their visual monitors for hundreds of years during their protracted interstellar communication, they saw the aliens as beautiful. The Alternans were humanoid, eight feet tall, lithe, and symmetrical. They were as near to perfection as the Tellusians could imagine without actually being Angels. Although the Alternans had no wings, as the Angels of Heaven do, they did possess a nimbus. And these haloes of yellow light impressed the Tellusians to no end because they believed the Alternans to be more advanced and even better than them. And they were flattered that these advanced aliens wanted to dialogue.

The beautiful Daughters of Tellus Mater believed in the ancient Greco-Roman paradigm of beauty where beauty equaled goodness and ugliness was akin to evil. But looking beautiful, if not pseudo-angelic, does not mean that you are good. And that is where the ancient paradigm from another time and world failed them. It was never meant to be an absolute as the Tellusians understood it. There were exceptions. Sometimes it simply was not applicable. It most certainly did not apply to the Alternans. But the Gabrielican Sisters of Atonement discovered the sad truth about the Alternans after it was too late.

Despite beauty, elegance, and apparent perfection, the Alternans were diseased. The entire race suffered from a genetic abnormality resulting in a metabolic disease that rendered them incapable of producing enough estrogen. And it was only by random chance that some of them discovered how to combat it.

To call the estrogen that they needed a craving diminishes the desire that the Alternans had for the sex hormone. Their so-called craving rendered them incapable of thinking logically. And, in some instances, it made them manic, obsessive, and utterly vicious.

Before the Alternans identified their metabolic shortfall, they were a short, wrinkled race with male attributes. What started them on the road to transformation was eating the ovaries of a domesticated feathered lizard from their world. It was called *Gallus*. Unknown to the Alternans, Gallus ovaries were riddled with estrogen. Eating Gallus ovaries made the Alternans smart. It altered their bodies. It changed the form of their offspring. And as long as they kept eating Gallus ovaries, they were in excellent mental and physical health.

In a single generation, Alterna became a society of two classes: the depleted and the supplemented. There were the Lodytes who dug for tubers, picked fruit when it was in season, and ate crustaceans and insects raw, who lived with their estrogen shortfall, as they had for thousands of years. And there were the Royal Houses of Alterna, the powerful and exceedingly rich who ate Gallus ovaries.

Then disaster struck. A plague swept across Alterna and made the Gallus sick. It made the Alternans sick too with pox. The Alternans survived the plague of chills, fever, and pustules. But the Gallus succumbed. A mass die off occurred. And within a fortnight the Gallus were extinct.

The rich looked elsewhere on the planet for another supplemental source of the unnamed elixir that made the Gallus ovaries so potent. They slaughtered every species possessing ovaries. But every creature fell short.

The powerful and the rich were in a conundrum because their so-called men of science, the alchemists of a primitive society more rooted in séance than science, were not advanced enough to identify, let alone replicate, the elixir in the Gallus ovaries that satisfied their needs. Suddenly, the privileged were faced with devolution and mental and physical impairment. And they did not want to return to the way they were. Who would? So, they looked elsewhere. They looked off planet. They sent messages to the stars, listened, and waited. Meanwhile, for generations, the privileged lived off of an exclusive stockpile of frozen Gallus ovaries kept in secret underground glacial bunkers in undisclosed locations around their world.

When the Alternans made first contact with the Tellusians and saw what the Daughters of Tellus Mater looked like, they were ecstatic. They saw the influence of an abundance of estrogen in their faces. It took years, decades, and centuries of contact truncated by space and time to discover that their first impressions were correct, that the Tellusians were a race of females brimming with the vital elixir that they craved.

The Children of Alterna invited the Daughters of Tellus Mater to their home world with open arms. And it was with great disappointment to the Alternans that the Tellusians proposed to send an initial expedition of only ten Gabrielican missionaries. The Children accepted nevertheless. Something was better than nothing. A tempting aroma, the tease of a taste, a miniscule bite sans satisfaction was better than no forbidden fruit at all.

The powerful and the rich of Alterna decided a hundred years before the arrival of the Tellusians how the precious sexual organs of their visitors would be vivisected, butchered, and distributed. For a time, the ovaries of the Gabrielican Sisters of Atonement were the most sought after commodity on the planet. And acquaintances of the lesser Royals spent fortunes to buy a seat at the oh-so-special dinner table to share in a piece of the Tellusian pie.

The Children had inquired discretely about the Tellusian population for hundreds of years before Gabrielican missionaries were sent to them. But instead of sending their harvesters to Tellus Mater even then to take what they needed, they waited to sample the goods. The Royal Houses of Alterna wanted to be sure.

To the Children, it was all about benefit versus cost. The Tellusian population numbered in the billions now and was large enough to make it economically worth their while. So, it all came down to the taste test and whether the Tellusian ovaries drugged them in the manner they required.

Esthetically, the Children had no problem vivisecting the Daughters. It didn't matter to them that the alien visitors were akin to new, lesser gods. To the Alternans, the Tellusians were little more than cows. They were a necessary inconvenience. Like a display case at the local delicatessen, the Daughters were organic receptacles containing the sweet meats and tasty treats that the Alternans craved.

It was merely a matter of giving the word and harvesters would be dispatched.

The journey from Alterna to Tellus Mater and back would be protracted but worth it in the long run. When the Children reached Tellus Mater, their mother ships would be positioned over the Tellusian cities. They would drug the air and the water. Then it was simply a matter of collection. Once the Tellusians were intoxicated, the Alternans would herd them aboard their harvesters where the Daughters would be vivisected on an industrial scale.

And weeks later, when their industrial operation closed, the Alternans would discard their last batch of Tellusians and return to their home world. The dead, diseased, and dying from the last vivisections would be scooped up in the shovels of front end loaders, like lifeless fish on ice, with frozen stares, in a seafood display case. And the offal would be dumped from open cargo bays from great heights, as the mother ships traversed the fluffy white, cumulous clouds of the cerulean sky on their leisurely mechanical ascendance to space. If the vivisected Daughters weren't dead when they were scooped, they would surely be dead when they hit the ground. And that would be that.

The mother ships would leave Tellus Mater with their cargo holds brimming with billions of flash frozen Tellusian ovaries. And the Alternans would return when, by their calculations, the Tellusian population had maximized itself again and ovaries were ready for harvest, even if it took ten thousand years.

Chapter 10 - salvation

What Mother Mary of the Gabrielican Sisters of Atonement saw, as she gazed through the transparent skin of Utera Kutuzov and viewed Alterna, at night, as the living starship neared the planet, were lights. There were lights everywhere. The Alternan Palace and the city that surrounded it were so lit up that they could be seen from space. Mary could clearly see all of the Alternan cities and the roads running between them. They looked like silver strings of gossamer studded with glistening raindrops against a field of black velvet.

Mary was glad that the ship was headed for the light because the dark frightened her. There were unknown creatures in the dark. Although she knew better and had been taught otherwise, she still associated the dark with danger, with evil, and with the Devil. It was the reason why she moved from the farm to the city when she was old enough.

She told herself that she moved to the city because country life was too boring, too quiet, and too static. She craved the city experience where there was something happening around the clock. She moved from the farm where everybody was asleep by eight and up at four to the city that never sleeps. She moved from the darkness of the farm where, on moonless and overcast nights, she couldn't see her hand in front of her face, where it was so dark that it was like being entombed, to the light dome and the night life of a megalopolis. She moved from the farm where, on clear nights, the one hundred and eighty degree dome of sky was lit with the ancient fire of billions of stars, and she was forced to contemplate her place in eternity, and felt as if she was falling upward into the abyss. And the abyss terrified her. So, she moved to the lights of the city with its washed out nighttime sky where the stars were out of sight and out of mind, and where she no longer had to look at them and feel frightened and insignificantly small. She moved to the city because she no longer had to contemplate eternity or feel the frightening and inevitable tug of death at her sleeve. She could dance and drink and carry on like there was no tomorrow because the only stars in her city existence were celebrities. And there was only the here and now.

The city was a drug. Mary was deeply addicted. And it overturned her sensibilities.

Mary deluded herself with her free and wild city life for several years. She got her university education there and pursued a career in xenolinguistics. She was very good at what she did. And she was as happy as a clam living in the hustle and bustle of the biggest city on Tellus Mater. It was called Yok. It was a phonetic derivation of a city from the Old Earth back when the planet and Les États-Unis existed.

Her life changed one afternoon in late autumn with a phone call informing her that her mother was dead. Mary travelled from Yok to her rural community and to the farm on which she grew up. She reacquainted herself with her family and old friends. And she buried her mother.

Mary spent three nights back on the farm. The first night, she refused to go outside when it was dark because she was overwhelmed by the hemisphere of sky that loomed over her and stretched from horizon to horizon in all directions. The second night, she went outside, looked up into the plethora of galaxies and stars everywhere, and prayed to God, even though she insisted that she no longer believed in God, to embrace and to protect the spirit of her mother. The third night, she was visited by an apparition that she took to be an Angel. And the deific Messenger showed her a paradigm that turned her world view upside down like Virgil surfacing from the Inferno.

The Angel showed her that the city, with its night sky so flooded by light that the stars were washed out, was evil. And it showed her that the starlit black sky of the country was good. The Angel told her that it was important for her kind to look at the stars. It informed her that the destiny of the human race rested in the stars and that the freedom of city life was an evil illusion that would result in the extinction of her kind. Moreover, the Angel told her that her one true calling was to serve God.

After a sleepless night of contemplation, pacing, and altogether too much coffee, Mary returned to Yok. And the next day, she applied to enter the Gabrielican Order.

The Royal House of Alterna, who gathered for the landing of Utera Kutuzov, salivated in anticipation like spiders prior to pouncing upon flies, while their prey buzzed wildly and dangled deliciously on their sticky webs. Queen Ingratia with her long raven hair and elegant white gown of bleached opalescent spider silk with bustle and train, and feet adorned with silk slippers attached to four foot stilts, sat upon her high throne at the forefront of the procession. And her bald-headed Princesses, Duchesses, Countesses, and Baronesses attired in colorful floor length lizard leather gowns, their feet adorned in wooden slippers carved into two foot stilts, as was the custom, sat at her sides upon thrones of varying height delineating their station in the royal hierarchy.

Beside them, as was also the custom in the matriarchy that ruled the planet, stood the King, Princes, Counts, and Barons in their long hair glued and pressed high over their heads like peacock tails, dressed in formal military attire of scarlet and blue with braids, brocade and buttons of gold, and conspicuous honors, medals, and titles fastened to their chests. On their feet they wore black leather, riding boots made from the back skin of Lodytes from the marshes, the unthinking brutes that they used to be before they discovered the benefits of eating Gallus.

The instant that Utera Kutuzov opened its portal on planet Alterna, Mother Mary of the Gabrielican Sisters of Atonement sensed that something was amiss. She looked out at the welcoming committee of Alternan Royals and everything looked normal enough for such an occasion. But looks can be deceiving, especially in the face of what the Tellusians all felt.

What Mary sensed coming from the Royals were waves of active electrolocation, like sharks used on the old Earth to zero in on their prey prior to the onset of a feeding frenzy. The waves made her ears ring. And they gave her a dizzying headache. She could tell, by looking at her associates, that the waves hit them too. The waves short-circuited their thinking, telepathic abilities, and extrasensory perception. It rendered them light sensitive, noise sensitive, and in pain.

But Mary and the others also sensed something piggybacked atop the waves. What they sensed was a hunger the likes of which they had never known. And the sheer power of the craving was unsettling. It bordered on mania. And when Mary looked at the smiling angelic faces of the beautiful Alternan Royals who were there to greet them, she was convinced that the waves came from them. She was also convinced that the transmissions were unintentional because who would consciously emit such thoughts. It gave them away. It revealed their dark secret. The Alternans were not what they seemed. It became clear to Mary and her sister nuns that the Alternans were predators and the Tellusians were the prey or perhaps the sacrifice.

A feeling of naked vulnerability swept over Mary. She stared at the palms of her hands. They had begun to bleed. And, as she stared at the scarlet stigmata, she came to a terrifying realization. She and the others were a long way from home. There was nobody there to protect them. And they were in great danger.

The others were terrified too.

Sister Philip fainted.

Sister Thaddeus, the youngest among them, peed through her habit noticeably and uncontrollably.

The Alternan Royals literally sensed the fear pouring from the Sisters with electroreceptors in their faces resembling the *ampullae of Lorenzini* found in sharks of the old Earth. They became agitated and animated because the jig was up. Their rouse was uncovered. The visitors sensed them sensing them. So, they moved quickly to restrain the nuns before they returned to the safety of their Utera and closed the portal, and the opportunity to partake of a delicacy was lost forever.

The Sisters were quite accurate to be worried about the Alternans. They were hungry on a level that the Gabrielicans could not image more akin to hormonal vampires than frenzied squamous. And their deceit had brought others to their planet for thousands of years.

The Children were not evil, as such, although their plot to lure the Tellusians could be considered evil. They didn't care who they deceived as long as their deception worked and lured prey to their doorstep. Prey was prey. And the message that the prey carried, the concept of it, was immaterial. To the Alternans, the *Book of Gabriel* and the Word of the Mother were the insignificant final moos of cows destined for the cooking pot. The religious words of the Sisters might just as well have fallen upon the ears of cannibals obsessed with thoughts of the alien soup that was to come and the frenzied flurry of sensation that its consumption would garner. The Children were just as egocentric and esthetically deaf.

The highly regimented matriarchy of Alterna forbade the use of written language except for the highest Royals themselves. And when they used written words, it usually took the form of laws or proclamations that few could comprehend let alone read written on the bleached and stretched skin of Lodytes. So, the *Book of Gabriel*, with its beauty, elegance, and grace was literally pearls before swine to a people who embraced the verbal tradition, had no education, and had no inclination to ever discern the Word of the Mother.

Even the Royals stared at the Book of Gabriel and did not know what to make of it. Prince Mark judged it by its cover, by its size, and by its weight as to how useful it might be. Count Anthony used it to balance a table. Baron Carter burned it for the few minutes of heat it generated, and considered it mostly useless. No one bothered to read it.

Despite verbal protest, the Tellusians were restrained and escorted to a dining hall reserved for the Royals of Alterna where a long table was set with finery. On other worlds, other Sisters were seated at similar receptions, regaled, toasted, and stuffed with the best drink and food that the alien world had to offer. But, on Alterna, the best that the home world had to offer at the sumptuous banquet were the guests themselves.

The ten Gabrielican Sisters of Atonement were not escorted to seats at the banquet table. Instead, they were forced to lie down upon T-shaped, large animal, dissecting tables borrowed from the biology labs at their most prestigious university and placed along the adjacent wood paneled wall. Their heads were positioned at the top of the T. Their arms were outstretched across the bridge of the T and fastened securely at the wrist. And their ankles were secured at the base. For all intents and purposes, they were prepared for crucifixion, sacrifice, or vivisection, spread out and tied down upon thin tables better suited to an anatomy class or to a surgical theater rather than to a banquet hall.

The Alternans showed the Gabrielicans no mercy despite their pleas. And they gave their prey no anesthetic prior to or during the procedure because it would taint the flavor of their oysters. The Alternan butchers pulled up the three dresses beneath the Gabrielican habits. They pulled up the long white undershirt. They cut off the white underpants, exposing the supple, young flesh. Then they sliced open the soft, down haired abdomens from hip to hip with knives better suited to a kitchen than to a hospital.

The butchers cut through abdominal muscles, pushed aside the intestines, and exposed the ovaries beneath. And when those in attendance smelled the Tellusian blood laced with adrenalin and estrogen, they became crazed with anticipation.

The ovaries were cut free and placed upon white paper doilies atop silver platters. And the white paper quickly stained scarlet. The confections were delivered across the room from dissection tables to the long banquet table with great pomp and circumstance. Then the steaming delicacies, fresh from the bodies of Tellusian virgins, were sliced paper thin by high priests and distributed to the special guests to be eaten bloody, raw, and warm.

The Children of Alterna looked upon the Sisters of Atonement as more than food, as more than snacks delivered to their door in an edible package. They saw them as deliverance, as manna from Heaven, as salvation.

And while the virgins bled scarlet into their abdominal cavities and thanked God that the worst of their excruciatingly horrifying and painful ordeal was over, the elite of Alterna, the estrogen vampires, the gourmands, thanked God for his generosity and consumed the sacred ovaries of the chosen ten they had waited so long to acquire. And their eyes rolled back in drugged ecstasy because, as promised, the mouthwatering treats were almost too sweet to eat.

Chapter 11 - zoë

The brightly lit Alternan banquet lasted through the evening and broke up in the wee hours of the morning. The alien delicacies were consumed first, washed down with alcohol distillate, and given Royal approval by Queen Ingratia, which determined the fate of Tellus Mater. Then the elite guests were regaled with diverse entertainment while they ate a thirty course meal and drank themselves more oblivious than usual.

The drunk and gluttonous Alternan Royals partied beneath the greenish light dome emitted from the Palace and its surrounding city. The light dome washed out the stars of the Milky Way and the dim smudges of billions of galaxies in the seventh universe. And that was the way the Royals liked it. They did not want to see the stars. It took away from their deemed self-importance. And they did not want their subjects to see the stars either or imagine life on trillions of other worlds orbiting those suns. They did not want them to think because thinking might lead to insurrection.

The Royals encouraged their people to live and work in the city where the elite could control the working class, and where the nighttime view of the starry heavens was obscured with light pollution. And so, with promises of freedom, people who were independent albeit subsistent in their rural environment migrated to the city where they were controlled and reliant. And those people who once believed in God when they lived in the swamp and could view the trillions of celestial objects in the night sky were corrupted into believing in Queen Ingratia in her opalescent gown, silk slippers, and stilts, and in the King in his scarlet military attire with gold brocade. The old beliefs of sending prayers up to Heaven on the wings of burning cinders flying up from their camp fires to the stars were painted as primitive and superstitious. And their old system of morals which instructed them to *do good* was replaced with the amoral idea: *do what feels good.*

At the break of dawn, the last of the satisfied Royals departed. The Grand dining Hall was cleared. And garbage attendants disposed of the trash.

The Alternans had no more use for the Gabrielicans. The Children had harvested the vital parts of the Daughters and what was left, in the opinion of the elite pseudo-Angels, was husk. It was offal. It was of no concern to them whether the missionaries died or lived, left the planet or stayed. Like autistics, the Alternans looked upon the depleted Gabrielicans as part of the background, as mere objects devoid of value. They no longer existed.

The injured nuns were transferred from dissection tables to gurneys. They were rolled out of the Grand Dining Hall and down a long hallway with high ceilings whose walls were lined with life size ancestral portraits of a Royal lineage going back five thousand years. Double doors were unlocked and thrown open. The gurneys were rolled across a large black granite terrace bordered by ornately carved balusters supporting a heavy top rail of the same cut, polished, and radioactive material with built in flower pots containing plants resembling tree philodendrons. And the vivisected Gabrielicans were thrown away with the half eaten carrots, peas, and potatoes from the sumptuous feast. They were lifted, one by one, over the railing and dropped unceremoniously into the feculent water of the steaming Grand Canal below to join the other organic trash. Then the gurneys were rolled away. The double doors were closed and locked. And that was that. The Daughters were out of sight and out of mind.

The Royal Palace and the city that surrounded it were built on piles driven deep beneath the swamps of Alterna until they hit granite. Upon that intrusive, felsic, igneous foundation the elite of Alternan civilization arose from its honest and humble beginnings as Lodytes. And, in doing so, it became perverse. But it was those surviving Lodytes, the estrogen depleted underclass, the have nots, who saved the ravaged Gabrielicans as best they could.

The Lodytes, ever vigilant to scrounge the culinary discards of Alternan feasts, paddled out into the shallow canal, in their primitive boats, to retrieve what they took to be garbage. But what they found were creatures so beautiful, so damaged by the elite, and so vulnerable that it broke their hearts. So, they gathered them gently and placed them in the protected interiors of their dugout canoes. They covered the delicate victims of the Royal cannibalism with large fronds to shield them from the harsh Alternan sun. And the Lodytes of Alterna transported the Daughters of Tellus Mater to their secluded camp deep within the swamp.

The Lodytes left behind the discarded food that they would have filled their boats with that day. Instead, their dugout canoes were filled with the damaged Gabrielicans that they found. For a day, they would starve. But it was worth it. It was the right thing to do for a people who saw that the discarded creatures were alien but human, and who sensed that the creatures believed in God, like them.

Mary was in and out of consciousness for three days. She passed out shortly after her vivisection. She remembered the lancinating pain of the procedure. And that was it. She awoke in a panic when she fell twenty feet and slapped the water of the canal. She remembered being pulled aboard a boat. She recalled the smell of lilacs. She saw the sun flickering through the tree tops. She remembered the sound of birds or lizards or monkeys howling all around her. And she awoke for a moment in a small grass hut, at nightfall, and saw an old woman illuminated by the flickering flame of a small fire. She remembered a wooden bowl with white syrup in it being pressed to her lips. And she drank because she trusted that the old woman who held the bowl was trying to help her.

The Lodyte woman's name was Armakeia. She was thirty years of age which was old by their standards. She was toothless, shrunken, and wrinkled, but otherwise in good health despite her hormonal deprivation. She had pulled out all of her own teeth when they became rotten from eating the sugared delicacies discarded by the Alternan elite. And she warned her tribe to abstain from the sweets. But they were addicted to the enticing treats and suffered from encroaching blindness, numbness, obesity, and rotten teeth too brought on by the black magic that the food of the Royals contained. She was at a loss to treat their difficulties. So, she drugged them with the smoke of the Sativa leaf to ease their pain.

Mary awoke only once, just before Armakeia's attempt to repair her. Her knees felt wet. And when she gazed down her body, past the three dresses of her habit and the long white undershirt beneath it that had all been pulled up around her waist and were stained brown with dried blood from the crude abdominal vivisection, she viewed fresh scarlet blood between her thighs. And she knew that she had spontaneously aborted her precious cargo. It was accident added to the injury of the Alternan assault. And despite her strength of will, Mary wept because the miscarriage was the final straw.

Mary wept because life was precious to her and the Sisters. She wept because her unborn daughter had already been given a name. And her name was Zeta-Omega-Eta or Zoë for short. It meant life. But there little Zoë was resting on her side between her mother's thighs, attached to umbilicus and ejected placenta amid a pool of scarlet blood, so blanched and small and still, dead before she had a chance to live, and wide eyed and staring into oblivion with thumb in mouth.

"Drink now," said Armakeia, as she stepped closer and placed a comforting palm on Mary's forehead. "It will take away your pain."

Mary stared into Armakeia's eyes and saw the eyes of her mother. And she drank the milky white syrup and fell unconscious.

Armakeia repaired what she could of the injured Gabrielican. She poured the fermented juice of swamp berries called Oxycoccus over her hands and over Mary's open abdominal wound. She delved within and saw what the Royal butchers had done to her. And the witch used the white hot tips of small straight sticks from her fire to cauterize the bleeders in Mary's abdomen. The witch arranged Mary's intestines properly so there were no obstructions. She located both sides of Mary's severed abdominal muscles and sewed them together with bone needle and a string of Silvestris gut soaked in fermented swamp berry juice. And when she was done, Mary was gusseted like a Christmas turkey ready for the oven.

Armakeia had no means of putting vital missing fluids back into Mary except by making her drink. And the witch awoke her periodically and lifted a bowl of pungent purple tea to her lips.

Every night, before the campfire was lit, the Lodytes looked up at the sky with dark-adapted eyes held wide open until they burned and tears streamed down their cheeks. And the longer they held open their eyes, the more they saw. Like magic, they saw the stars of the Milky Way and the distant galaxies behind them appear from the blackness of the heavens, where nothing was there moments before, in numbers too great to count or to imagine. And they were in awe of God the Creator of Alterna and the heavens.

So, the Lodytes, which meant *the people who know and know they know* in their language, were grateful and humble before the Lord.

66

They thanked God for creating the Lodyte people. They thanked God for giving them eyes with which to look. And they thanked God for giving them brains with which to see.

Intuitively, Armakeia believed that each twinkle in the night sky was a sun. She believed that around each sun there spun a world like her own. And she believed that, just as she pondered life on other worlds, creatures on other worlds pondered her, and stared at the twinkle of the Alternan sun and contemplated her contemplating them as she squatted, like a frog, at the campfire in the Lodyte swamp.

Armakeia sat at the campfire with the tribal elders, chanted, prayed for the recovery of the damaged Gabrielicans in their midst, and talked. When the elders were all talked out, they sat quietly, stared into the fire, and remembered the exploits and foolishness of their youth. And when the campfire finally burned itself down to red coals, and their bones ached from the late night chill, the others limped off to beds warmed by wives. But Armakeia remained.

With her dark-adapted eyes, the Lodyte holy woman and witch gazed upward into the sparkling heavens and contemplated eternity. She contemplated the life and death of her people, her own birth and eventual demise, the creation and death of suns, and whether God created herself and would eventually succumb. And after three nights of chanting, and prayers flung up to the heavens on the wings of flying embers, and the contemplation of eternity, Mary finally regained consciousness.

The Gabrielican surfaced with the red sun at morn as it burned through the rotten egg fog hanging above the shimmering waters of the Lodyte swamp. She was weak, in excruciating agony, and felt more nauseated than she had ever known. Her blood pressure was low due to blood loss despite Armakeia's attempts to replace her fluids with purple tea. And her sugar was dangerously low. Yet, despite dizziness, impaired vision, tremors, sweating, and confusion, Mary had the wherewithal to call Misha in her mind. And Utera Kutuzov took off in a panic from where she had touched down days before within the grounds of the Royal Palace.

Misha had not heard from Mary or the others for three days and was beside herself with worry. And she flew to Mary in the swamps of Alterna as fast as her thoughts would take her, and landed on the grounds of the primitive village near Armakeia's grass hut atop a large curved dome of weathered black granite.

Tellusian Seed by Mark Carter

The villagers were in awe of Utera Kutuzov when she landed in their midst because they had never seen anything fly that was her size. For a time, they surrounded her and watched. They were not afraid of her, only cautious and curious. They watched her breathe. They observed her looking at them through eyes that looked intelligent and kind. And they heard her purr. And that was it. Their hearts melted. They approached her. And although she was vastly different from anything they had previously known, they adopted her as a friend on the spot and spread their arms wide. They hugged the behemoth who had landed in their midst and transmitted their feelings of love. And outside of her own kind, Misha had never known such open and honest affection. Misha was moved emotionally. She purred like a satisfied cat and sent kaleidoscopic colors rippling across her skin. And everyone was amazed and delighted.

Armakeia and her assistant helped Mary get from the grass hut to the living starship. A portal opened as they approached. And when Armakeia entered, she was amazed at how bright it was. White light without heat seemed to come from the walls themselves. It seemed to come from everywhere. But she was even more amazed by the magic that came next.

The other Daughters were carried into the starship shortly after by young male villagers. The men were thanked, asked to leave, and left. Armakeia was asked to stay, if she wished, to observe. She accepted the invitation. And the portal sealed.

Mary cried for Misha to help her, and the projection of the Utera appeared in Mary's mind. Misha appeared in Armakeia's mind too. Alarmed by Mary's weakness, Misha created a chair for her to sit in. It morphed from the deck beneath her and scooped her up. And Armakeia was amazed.

"I am so thirsty," said Mary.

And Misha provided Mary with emergency oral electrolyte and saw to it that the Tellusian drank it. Then Mary requested an intravenous catheter, pole, and lines, and Misha made them materialize too. And Armakeia was amazed once again.

Mary sanitized the back of her left hand with alcohol and iodine. She opened a sterile 16 gauge IV needle hooked to a cannula and inserted the needle into a peripheral vein. She removed the metal trocar. And Armakeia was beside herself. It was obvious to the native healer that Mary was a witch with great magic. And she was grateful to be there. So she did what she was told and helped out where she could. She followed Misha's lead and hung bags of antibiotics, dextrose, pain medication and saline onto the hook of a mobile IV pole. And she watched as Mary hooked up the lines to a shunt, and set the flow to fast. Then the injured Mother Superior, pulling IV pole beside her, saw to the needs of the others. And Armakeia went with her.

Misha metamorphosed the deck beneath the Gabrielicans into beds. And, as Mary walked from patient to patient, she saw that the situation was dire. To her horror, they had all miscarried. Six of the nuns were dead, including Sister John who was her assistant and best friend. And four were alive but unconscious and terribly dehydrated.

The deceased died in their sleep between day one and three from blood loss and shock sustained from the grotesque culinary procedure performed upon their virginal flesh to satisfy the perverse gustatory pleasures of the Alternan elite. If Armakeia had been able to give them intravenous electrolytes during that time, they might have survived. But that level of medicine was far beyond her primitive witchcraft.

Armakeia was not the cause of their demise despite the rough surgery that she performed to save them with stone knife, bone needle, and preserved Silvestris gut. Yet, all she felt was sadness. She had failed them all. And she stared at her useless hands. If only her hands knew more. If only she had better magic, they would be alive.

Mary placed a reassuring hand on Armakeia's shoulder to quiet her, and said, "It's not your fault." And Armakeia nodded. She knew. But tears streamed down her cheeks nonetheless.

The four remaining nuns were unconscious. Misha created blankets and Armakeia covered them. Misha created intravenous poles and hanging cocktails similar to Mary's for them. And Mary hooked them up. She took their blood pressure. And she examined their wounds without opening Armakeia's rough sewing that held them shut for fear of extending their bleeding.

Then Mary prayed. And Armakeia got down on her knees and prayed too.

Mary felt abused. She felt betrayed. She felt raped. Moreover, she felt stupid. How had the Tellusians not seen or sensed the true motives of the Alternans? How had she not noticed? She was responsible for the crew of Utera Kutuzov. All but two of them, her assistant and herself, were novitiates, babies in training, and utterly trusting in her guidance and protection. And she had let them down. She, Mother

Mary of the Gabrielicans Sisters of Atonement, had let all of her babies down.

And Mary was furious. Her thoughts, then and there, were so dark that, had it been possible, she would have crucified the Alternans who attended the banquet. She would have crucified every pseudo-Angel on the planet and elsewhere. And when all was said and done, she would have picked up the planet itself, raised it over her head, and heaved the inhospitable world into the fiery orange furnace of their star. And even that did not seem enough.

Then Mary caught herself. She looked at Armakeia and sighed. The primitive witch watched her every move with wide-eyed wonderment. There was compassion, sensitivity, and intelligence in those eyes. How could she condemn an entire planet when Armakeia and her people had such eyes? So, Mary thought better thoughts.

"Help me," moaned Sister Bartholomew, as the saline drip revived her. "Help me."

And Mary was by her side immediately, despite her own discomfort and weakness. She placed her right hand on the frightened girl's forehead and whispered her secular name to comfort her.

"I'm here, Anne," she said. "You're going to be all right."

"It hurts," whined the young woman, who was hardly more than a baby herself.

"I know it does, darling," whispered Mary, as she injected a small push of morphine into the shunt in Anne's left hand. "I want you to go back to sleep. Okay?"

"Okay."

Mary checked Sister Bartholomew's temperature. She was burning up. She felt her abdomen. It was rigid and uneven. So, she decided to go back in. Armakeia's primitive surgery was a valiant attempt. But she had missed things. Mary was sure of it. So, she operated on Sister Bartholomew to correct.

With Misha's assistance, and with Armakeia observing, Mary operated on Anne to ensure that she survived. She gave her a push of Twilight. Then she removed the unsanitary gusseting. She retracted the crude incision. She moved aside a jumble of Anne's bloodied and knotted small intestines destined to eventually obstruct her and kill her. She flushed and sucked out the coagulated blood from where it had settled at the bottom of the abdominal cavity. She cauterized the broad ligament, from which the ovaries were excised, the ovarian blood vessels responsible for the bleeds, and the damaged *Ostium abdominale*. Then Mary carefully unknotted the jumble of small intestines and positioned them properly. She searched for the *Rectus abdominis* that had been sliced, had rolled up like window blinds, and had never been re-joined adequately, and sutured them together tightly while leaving a small hole for a drainage tube. She closed the skin with titanium staples. She hung extra saline, dextrose, and antibiotics. And that was that. Misha placed her in a secluded place to recover from surgery and would monitor her carefully until she was on her feet again.

Mary performed similar surgeries to correct on the three others to ensure their survival too. She needed to have corrective surgery herself, and would once the dead were dispatched with dignity. Anne, the others, and Mary would eventually make it back to Tellus Mater. But the six dead girls were not so lucky. They were destined to remain, for all time, on the world that greeted their kind arrival with cruel vivisection.

Mary worked diligently and respectfully, despite the aroma, to prepare the bodies of the dead to rest in peace. She owed them that much. After three exposed days in the subtropical heat, the girls were ripe with the sickly green smell of death.

One by one, Mary removed the bloody habits of the dearly departed of her Order. She sponged away the encrusted blood with soap and water. She dried them. She combed their hair. And she dressed them in fresh habits. She cut the fetuses free from their umbilical cords, washed the small creatures, wrapped them, and placed them over the hearts of their mothers. She crossed the hands of her beloved Gabrielican Sisters, wrapped Rosaries around their wrists, and placed holy books in their hands. She filled their mouths with cotton so their cheeks did not look sunken. She sewed shut their lips. She gave their faces and hands color so that they looked alive in death. And lastly, she draped muslin over their faces to keep away the insects.

Then Mary prayed for them. She prayed that God forgive them their sins and accept their souls. It was an old prayer from an old time on the old Earth that was still used in the sisterhood. She anointed the foreheads of her departed Sisters with olive oil blessed by the Bishop of their Order on Maundy Thursday. She anointed Sister Andrew with *Oleum Infirmorum*, and said, "Through this holy unction may the Lord pardon thee whatever sins or faults thou hast committed." And

71

likewise, she performed Extreme Unction over Sister John, Matthew, Peter, Philip, and Simon.

When Mary was done, she nodded to Armakeia. And the Lodyte witch, with great respect for Mother Mary, and with great reverence for the deceased, punched a small hole through the crown of the dead Gabrielicans to allow their souls a means of egress to the next life. And with equally great solemnity, she pierced the pliable temples of the fetuses with a knife sanctified for the occasion. Then she squashed a ripe Oxycoccus berry onto the forehead of each nun to speed their souls on their way to the next life, as was the custom of her people. And that was that. She called the others, and the nuns were carried away.

Mother Mary was permitted to sit through the solemn Lodyte ceremony to release the souls of the dead because she was still weak from her ordeal and the deceased belonged to her. Everyone else stood. The entire tribe stood out of respect.

Funeral pyres of precious wood were built to the east of the village, facing the rising sun, on an upwelling of smooth, black, aphanitic, igneous rock littered with conflagrated bones and teeth from generations of cremations. It was considered the holiest place in the Lodyte domain. It was the sacred burial ground of a people who lived on a world of swamps that had no place where the dead could be buried. It was the final resting place of generations. It was a place of good-byes and memories. It was their place of cremation. And Mary was honored that the Lodytes were willing to share the sacred site and the secret ceremony with her.

The six deceased Gabrielicans, with *The Holy Bibl*e clasped in their right hands and the *Book of Gabriel* held in their left, with Rosary beads wrapped around their wrists and swaddled fetuses placed over their hearts, were carried, by villagers, from Utera Kutuzov to individual funeral pyres with great solemnity. And they were positioned softly and respectfully atop the geometrical stacks of wood.

Armakeia uttered the sacred words of her tribe that honored the dead. And when she was done, Mary uttered a small prayer asking the Mother of Creation to watch over the souls of her departed Sisters. Chests heaved. Tears fell. And in the distance, Misha moaned.

Armakeia handed Mary a flaming torch, and she did what had to be done. Mary blinked, at first, crossed herself, and said, "Mother, give me strength." Then she walked from pyre to pyre, and set the cashew ablaze. The dried wood caught quickly, burned fast, hot, and yellow, and put out white smoke. Flames licked the Tellusian bodies and accelerated. Flesh crackled and fat dripped. The incinerated complex carbohydrates, lipids, and proteins turned the smoke black. The rancid and sickly sweet smell of burning death eddied across the swamp. And the souls of the six dead girls departed.

Armakeia, Mary, and the Lodytes watched the funeral pyres burn for two hours. Then the villagers walked the injured Gabrielican nun back to her starship. And Armakeia and Mary said good-bye.

Armakeia took off the leather necklace and carved bone pendant that she wore and hung it upon Mary. And Mary, in turn, removed her heavy necklace and crucifix of gold and hung it on Armakeia. Mary hugged and kissed the witch, and said, "Good-bye, my friend, and thank-you." The shriveled women reached out desperately, grasped Mary's right hand, and kissed it. And both women went red in the face with embarrassment.

The Tellusian nun waved to the villagers that had escorted her back to her starship and had stayed to wish her farewell. And they returned the friendly gesture. The Reverend Mother gave the Alternan Lodyte witch one last bright white smile before retreating into the starship. And Armakeia smiled back with her purple, missing, and rotten teeth. Then the portal closed. The spacecraft released a high-pitched electromagnetic wail. The crowd stepped back. And Utera Kutuzov jumped abruptly into the blue Alternan sky, and was gone.

Misha leaped into space with a thought and used the Alternan sun to lens her to the next star on a protracted journey back to the Sol system. And as Misha lensed, Mary viewed Alterna through the Utera's transparent skin, as she had when they approached, and watched the planet as it shrunk and quickly disappeared.

The Alternan Royals were not the Angels that they appeared. Yet they were not Devils either, in the traditional sense. They were amoral parasites, manipulators, and sociopaths. They were utterly disingenuous. They were non-believers and had no intention of learning anything from the *Book of Gabriel* or from the Gabrielicans. When their planet vanished, Mary spit out her venom. Then she quickly apologized to Misha for her rudeness. But the Utera understood and did not take the insult personally.

Ironically, it was the Lodytes, the people of the swamps, the deformed, hormonally deprived and ugly half of the Alternan race, the true believers, who were the real Angels of Alterna or would be

73

eventually. And the Gabrielican Mother was grateful to be alive. If not for Armakeia's primitive surgery and purple tea, Mary was convinced that she would have joined her unfortunate babies who succumbed to the inhumane Alternan ordeal.

As per Mary's instructions, Misha broadcast the dilemma that the Gabrielicans experienced on Alterna, at the speed of thought, across the galaxy to her Uteran sisters. And they saw to it that the message got to Tellus Mater as soon as possible. But, even then, it took decades.

As Utera Kutuzov lensed between the stars, Mary operated on herself. With Misha's assistance, she flushed away her blood clots, cauterized her cut and torn blood vessels, rearranged her bowels, re-joined her stomach muscles, and placed a drainage tube. Then, she juiced herself with Morphine and slept, like Anne and the others, while Misha watched over them all.

The day after Utera Kutuzov and its beautiful but injured Gabrielicans departed from the Lodyte village deep in the Alternan swamp, the Stone Age life of Armakeia and her people resumed.

The young men and women of the tribe journeyed through the rotten egg reek of the pre-dawn fog, in their dugout canoes, to the canal at the foot of the Royal Palace where they awaited the culinary discards of the elite that the Lodytes used to supplement their simple subsistence diet of crustaceans, grubs, and berries. At mid-morning, the Royal kitchen of Queen Ingratia wheeled the culinary discards from morning breakfast to the high balcony of the palace. The manna was dumped into the feculent opaque water of the canal below. The Lodytes scrambled to retrieve as much as they could. And by noon, when the sulfur dioxide fog burned off, the polluted water of the canal was devoid of culinary refuse. And the Lodytes were on their way home with dugout canoes loaded high with vegetable cuttings, half eaten meals, and pristine entrees thrown away simply because they had grown cold.

When the canoes arrived at the village, the culinary extravagance was evenly distributed. The very old and the very young were fed before the others. And so, a barefoot girl ran through the village with a small wicker basket containing cheese, tuber peelings, and orange colored roots, and placed the bounty at the entrance to Armakeia's hut.

The witch retrieved the manna, and was grateful. But, as she picked through the tuber peelings, she was stopped in her tracks and forced down upon her knees to pray. She didn`t know how or why or why her. But there it was. Beneath the cuttings was a waterlogged tome bearing a rune that she recognized. She grasped the pendant given to her by Mary that hung around her neck by a chain. The rune and the pendant were one and the same.

Armakeia dried out the saturated tome and stored it, but she was not able to comprehend it for ten years. When she was toothless and ancient, the Royals passed legislation ordering all Lodyte children to attend school and learn how to read and write so they could work for the elite as an underclass with basic skills. And it was the children of her village who taught the *old mother*, as Armakeia was known by then, how to read Alternan.

Armakeia opened her warped copy of the *Book of Gabriel*, in translation, dragged the wrinkled index finger of her right hand over the opening words, and sang Gabriel's deep, throbbing mantra as a joyous, rising, octaval chant. "I'm CLEAN," she sang. And Alternan destiny smiled upon the Lodytes on their rocky road to God.

On the heels of Utera Kutuzov's departure, and in a decision based on benefit versus cost, the Royal Houses of Alterna launched their harvesters toward the pale blue dot.

Decades passed before Tellus Mater discovered that their missionaries to Alterna had been vivisected. And they wept that six had died from the cruel and unusual ordeal. But, even then, the epiphany that the Alternans were disingenuous was unbelievable to many. Some Tellusians insisted, despite the facts, that the Alternans were absolutely good. Others accused them of being utterly evil. After seemingly endless discussions, the Daughters compromised and classified the Alternans as ambivalent but dangerous. They transmitted a final message to the Alternans delineating their displeasure. Then they ceased all communications, and sent no further missions there. And that, to the Daughters, was that.

But it was not the end of the matter to the Alternans. To them, the reaction of the Tellusians was expected and laughable because of the verisimilitudes of space and time. The Children had been through it before with other species. And by the time they got the Tellusian response to the Gabrielican vivisections, their further actions were already decades in the making. The ball was still in play. The Tellusians just didn't realize it. And they wouldn't until it was too late.

Chapter 12 - hell

The Rancorian home world was dotted with gas and oil wells as far as the eye could see. For hundreds of years the inhabitants had lived off of the ancient energy stored within the sedimentary rocks set down millions of years before during their planet's lengthy carboniferous period.

Mining the coal, oil, and natural gas gave the Rancorians the ability to create and to maintain a vast planet-wide city. Hydrocarbons from the past provided them with the energy of the present. It drove their machines through the air, across the land, and upon and beneath the waters of their world. It propelled them into space and beyond. But the energy came at a price.

The Rancorians were once a beautiful people. They were once lithe, tall bipedal humanoids similar to the humans of Tellus Mater but of a different origin. They were once soft spoken and of a kind disposition. There was a time, so it is said, when they believed in God the Creator of all things.

But the mining of hydrocarbons changed all of that. Now they believed in money, science, and technology. They believed in the infinite possibilities of organic chemistry. Although the carcinogens, mutagens, and teratogens associated with fracking, oil drilling, and petrochemical refining made them deformed, diseased, and stunted, they chalked it up to the price of doing business.

Their attitude had become just as corrupt as their bodies. They hated themselves. They hated life. And wherever they saw beauty flourish on their home world, they snuffed it. They hydraulically fractured more shale. They drilled another oil well. They dug up more tar sands from massive open pits. They released so much sulfur dioxide into the atmosphere that the indigenous flora and fauna perished, concrete corroded, and everyone developed chronic chemical pneumonia. Their obsession with hydrocarbons transformed their world into one continuous field of oil derricks and pumps, pipelines, refineries, and vents. They made a Hell of their world without knowing what Hell was.

So, when they encountered Tellusians through their radio messages searching the Milky Way galaxy for intelligent life, the Rancorians wanted nothing more than to destroy them too. The Tellusians sounded altogether too nice. The Rancorians gulled the Tellusians into sending missionaries to their home world with false radio transmissions that misrepresented themselves. Meanwhile, they sent a fleet of warships to Tellus Mater to transform it into a Hell on Earth.

The Rancorian path to corruption started with the invention of the hydronium hydroxide vapor engine: a device that burned cellulose to boil dihydrogen monoxide to create heated vapor that pushed a piston to turn a wheel. Beasts of burden were replaced overnight by machines that did the work of several of them at once whose only demands were cellulose, oil and dihydrogen monoxide. The engine transported the Rancorians around their planet. It opened up frontiers. And it powered the wheels and pulleys of industry.

Cracking oil into its constituents led inevitably to another type of engine, one that ignited volatile liquid hydrocarbons within an enclosed, reinforced space to propel a piston that cranked a shaft that turned a wheel. It was a smaller, lighter engine. And the Rancorians were able to place it in more devices. It allowed them to travel upon and beneath the waters of their world. It allowed them to travel everywhere upon the ground once flat conglomerate corridors were constructed to accommodate the vehicles they created for ground transportation. And the liquid hydrocarbon engine allowed them to fly.

The Rancorian love affair with hydrocarbons went on for hundreds of years. Ninety per cent of their world was underlain with deposits. It was abundant and easily accessible. Hydrocarbons pervaded the Rancorian civilization and mindset. It drove their market economy. It powered their electrical grid. It boiled hydronium hydroxide for their four o'clock chai.

So, when nay sayers spoke out against hydrocarbons, as the occasional insane Rancorian did, they were shot down. Rancorians shook their heads when these insane types ranted about using proton, star, or zephyr energy instead of hydrocarbons. When they became an embarrassment, these insane creatures were accused of purveying naked pictures of young Rancorians and that accusation usually worked to discredit them. If they persisted, they received a knock on the door in the middle of the night, which meant it was bashed in, and they were taken. They were never seen again. Everyone knew that the Hydrocarbon Conglomerate was behind it. And behind the Conglomerate was the government of Rancor itself. But no one dared to speak up about it for fear of being taken themselves.

Once, a long time ago, the Rancorian civilization was agrarian. But since the discovery of hydrocarbons and the advent of their industrial revolution, and the perpetual increase in their population, rural had become urban more and more until a city stretched across the globe and there was no longer farm land to grow food on. Vegetables were grown vertically in massive greenhouses covering thousands of square miles, as an intermediary step. But the greenhouses could not keep up with demand. So, like everything else, food was manufactured on a massive industrial scale, in mega-factories, from the oil that Rancor had in abundance.

And waste was recycled. It was too valuable to merely throw away and bury in dumps as they had in the past. Garbage was recycled. It was mostly plastic. So it was sorted by type, ground, and reused in hot press manufacturing. Feces and urine were recycled. Shit was processed for the vital iron it contained, and worked back into the food system. Salt and urea and were extracted from pee, microorganisms were filtered, and the remaining liquid was worked back into the drinking water system. And when Rancorians died, their bodies were recycled too.

No one among the plebeians knew precisely what deceased Rancorians were recycled into. Some guessed that they were broken down and plasticized. They guessed that the slurry from dead bodies was heat pressed into grocery bags. Some guessed that they were vacuum-formed into hot tubs. So much of modern Rancorian civilization was made of plastic that most plebeians guessed some kind of plastic when asked the question. Many people speculated that their deceased loved ones were emulsified, filtered, artificially colored, mixed with vitamins and minerals, and heat pressed into wafers containing the proper proportions of carbohydrates, lipids, and proteins.

They were available everywhere under different names and in different wrappers, but they were essentially the same.

Everyone died. Everyone was recycled. No one starved on Rancor. Waste not. Want not.

Chapter 13 - encounters

When Deesha was young, she asked: "What is the meaning of life?" And she was chastised by her mother for being an impudent daughter.

"You are a foolish child who does not yet understand that life is the meaning," said her mother. "Amid the vastness of space and time, where there exists so much cold and emptiness between remote islands of extreme heat in a tumultuous galaxy amid millions of similarly violent galaxies in the universe, that fragile and precious rarity that we call life is to be cherished above all. We Uterans know this. Others, whenever and wherever they are, including a young Uteran child named Deesha, might eventually come to know it too."

As Deesha grew older, she came to understand that all life was fragile and precious, in whatever form it took, however it presented itself, and despite the label that was imposed upon it. Life simply was. It evolved from the physical despair of the universe. It was the answer to the question, "Is that all?"

Having evolved as far as corporeal beings could, the Uterans considered it their duty to altruistically give back. So, in the spirit of *noblesse oblige*, they spread life throughout the galaxy. They seeded damaged, dead, and dying solar systems, whose planets were decimated by meteor impacts, planetary collisions, and solar flares, with the fundamental bio-matter from which life would eventually spring to give those systems a second chance. And they hoped that someday and somewhere their good deeds would be noticed by God.

Long before Utera Lysanderos committed herself to a symbiotic relationship with the Daughters of Tellus Mater, long before she began her journey toward Rancor so that her friends could spread the Word of the Mother through the *Book of Gabriel*, she roamed the Milky Way, as did her remote sisters, spreading the seed of life in her search for God. And, upon occasion, amid the deep emptiness and emotional loneliness of interstellar space, she encountered another traveler. And, as they approached each other on the same trajectory, at the speed of lens and light, they acknowledged one another and communicated briefly. It began with salutations.

"I am Uteran. My name is Deesha. Who are you?"

"I am Gaian. My name is Triandafilo."

Deesha saw into Triandafilo's mind and viewed the beautiful image of a red rose when she said her name. Her name was Rose. And the thought of it pleased Deesha greatly.

And, in turn, Triandafilo read Deesha's mind and saw that Deesha's name meant violet in the Uteran language. Her name was Violet of God. And the knowledge pleased Triandafilo on several levels.

"Why are you here?" asked Rose.

"I spread God's seed among the stars," said Deesha. "What about you?"

"I do the same."

"That gives me great joy."

"It pleases me as well."

"We are each going where the other had been. Let us share information to avoid duplication."

"I agree."

And in the few moments before the crafts passed each other in the darkness, navigational and other information was pulsed between the ships, so that they might share where they had been, what they had done, and more precisely who they were. And just before the Doppler shift of their passing made communication difficult and then impossible, the starships wished each other good-bye and good luck.

"Farewell Violet of God, my Uteran friend."

"God be with you in your travels, my Gaian friend, Rose."

The radio noise rose to a crescendo then fell off sharply, crackled, and sputtered to silence, as the approaching light ships came out of the darkness and flashed past each other. Their appearance shifted from blue to red. They vanished into darkness once again. The inky blackness and loneliness of the interstellar night rushed in to fill the wake. And, except for the data that the new found friends transmitted to each other, it was as if they had never been.

Now, as Deesha lensed toward Rancor to deliver her precious cargo of Gabrielican nuns on their mission of peace, she encountered many light ships in a cluster. She greeted them as they approached, but the ships did not return her hail. As they neared, she sensed only emptiness and death coming from them. She sensed cold, dark metal propelled by pulses of superheated plasma. She sensed the cold logic of sleeping computers and the absence of thought coming from unconscious passengers entombed in cylinders of liquid nitrogen awaiting revival. And her heart sank.

As Deesha approached the ships at the speed of lens and light, she hoped for a brief Doppler conversation, a greeting amid the darkness, a simple hello between travelers, in passing. But their klystron-pumped plasma engines were set to full throttle, electronically accelerating hydrogen ions to millions of degrees, and blasting them into space with stellar fury. And the unknown travelers flashed by without acknowledgment. And, if it is possible for Uteras to sigh and be heard in the emptiness of interstellar space, she was.

Deesha heard herself sigh from within herself. And throughout the galaxy her Uteran sisters heard her sigh too because she couldn't help but telepathically broadcast her strong emotions. Her encounter with the unknown ships was more than merely rude. It was more than intelligent, organic life encountering an inert, deep space object like a chunk of rock. What she encountered were mechanical creations built by intelligent creatures and possessing some level of sentience. Like other travelers, they should have been programed to elicit some response when hailed. But they had been switched off. And Deesha wondered why. She found the encounter frustrating and puzzling. All mechanisms were built for a purpose. And Utera Lysanderos wondered whether the purpose of the unknown travelers was evil.

She had counted one hundred starships of similar make and model as they approached and flashed past like lightning amid the perpetual night. In her mind's eye, she could see them. They were unlike her sister Utera or herself. They did not flash messages at each other on skins that changed with their emotions. They did not speak to one another telepathically. Except for proximity sensors that kept them from running into each other, and into objects that they approached, they were inert, nonliving, non-sentient mechanisms that looked like large, black scorpions.

Deesha calculated where the scorpions were headed, and it did not bode well. They were curving through space and time toward a solar system near the inner rim of the Orion arm of the Milky Way galaxy that was not yet there, but would be by the time the armada arrived. And her heart sank because she sensed that the scorpions were bringers of death and destruction, and they were heading toward Tellus Mater.

Chapter 14 - landings

Athousand years of radio communication back and forth between Rancor and Tellus Mater had convinced the Tellusians that the oil world would be receptive to diplomatic discourse, to the Word of the Mother, and to the teachings of Gabriel. So, on that day of days when a thousand starships ventured into the Milky Way to spread the Word, it was Sophia and her Gabrielican Sisters of Atonement who journeyed to Rancor.

But a thousand years is a long time. Policies and politics change. Whereas the Tellusians were once invited to Rancor, now they were uninvited. But the Rancorians did not inform the Tellusians of their change in politics. In fact, and insidiously so, the Rancorians continued their beguiling dialogue as the ship designated to land on Rancor approached.

The Tellusians asked for permission to enter Rancorian space, at the rocky outskirts of their system. And they were granted access. They asked for permission to orbit the alien world, as they drew closer, and they were granted that too. They were instructed where to land, and the Tellusians followed the Rancorian instructions faithfully. But it was all a ruse. As Utera Lysanderos entered the atmosphere on final approach to the designated landing site in the desert, the Tellusian starship was attacked.

The Rancorians fired two Black Tongue missiles at Utera Lysanderos. The ground-to-air, heat-seeking, solid propellant devices were equipped with explosive payloads and a ninety mile range. Deesha avoided the first projectile by increasing velocity and changing direction. But it only brought her closer to the second which detonated, by proximity, a millisecond before hitting her starboard nacelle. It took a split second for the initial missile to see her damaged and burning metallic body with its infrared sensors, and to reacquire its target. And that was it. There was nothing Deesha could do to stave off the inevitable, as the missile came up quickly from behind for a second try. She and her passengers merely had time to brace themselves before the impact and detonation blew Deesha's aft to smithereens.

A flurry of blinding white burning magnesium debris from her aft joined the debris from her damaged nacelle in a slow dance of fire and white smoke that arced across the deep blue upper atmosphere toward the horizon and an inevitable collision with terra firma. What remained of Deesha herself spun round and around, and quite out of control because of the engine imbalance, burning brilliant and hot, emitting white smoke, sparking, and sputtering as she arced along the same trajectory toward a similar fate a little further downrange.

Deesha's sophisticated electronic defenses, installed by the Tellusians to augment her natural systems, were on standby mode when the Rancorian missiles approached and hit. All she had to go by were her ancient Uteran instincts to avoid predators, which she still possessed from a time when creatures of her kind were cuttlefish in a tepid sea. But ancient organic instincts were no match for the processing speed of modern Rancorian electronics. So, she succumbed to the assault. And the Tellusian mission to Rancor was over before it began.

Deesha was hurt physically by the missile attack. She quickly assessed her damage and sensed that it was catastrophic. She still had the ability to make a rough landing. But her Tellusian passengers would never survive it. So, she jettisoned the capsule in which they sat strapped in and unconscious from the ten G flat spin she was in.

The capsule was a Tellusian addition to her being. When Hephzibah introduced the Daughters of Tellus Mater to the Uterans and suggested a symbiotic relationship, the Tellusians requested that some of their own nuts and bolts technology be incorporated into the little understood organic technology of the behemoths. And the Uterans begrudgingly accepted the modifications to their bodies for the privilege of being loved by the Tellusians and journeying with them throughout the Milky Way in their mutual quest to find God. The alterations to their precious bodies were a small price to pay.

Deesha communicated with the computer aboard the Tellusian capsule and informed it of her catastrophic damage. And the capsule activated its Atmospheric Entry Emergency Protocol. The program

86

launched an emergency buoy designed to travel into low planetary orbit and to broadcast a distress signal that would take altogether too many years to be of any real help. Explosive bolts that held the capsule to Deesha's frame blew in rapid succession. A brief rocket burst separated the ships. With a jolt, the capsule unclamped, unplugged, and slipped free from the rapidly spinning, organic starship. And the autopilot took control of the attitudinal rockets and quickly stabilized the small re-entry craft as it fell like a brick through the upper atmosphere.

Sophia regained consciousness before the others just in time to see Violet of God through the fore starboard viewing port in front of her. She watched in awe, reverence, and silence as above and beyond them all, on fire and spewing white smoke, sparkling bright like Venus against the dark blue sky before sunrise, the beloved vessel and living starship that had been their friend, home, and sentient protector during their journey across the stars spun out of control and plummeted wildly toward the horizon on a ballistic track across the upper atmosphere of Rancor.

"Deesha," cried Sophia. But the ship made no telepathic reply. And the Tellusian feared that her Uteran friend was dead.

The falling capsule hit the boundary layer of the Rancorian atmosphere shortly after. The rarefied ionization obscured Sophia's view of Deesha. And the ride turned bumpy and hot.

The capsule vibrated violently as it ripped through the ozone layer. And Sophia clenched her teeth so they wouldn't chatter. She wondered whether she and her Gabrielicans would survive. Then, when she least expected it, she heard her name. She thought it was Deesha calling to her, all alone and miles away, entering the atmosphere herself. And Sophia's heart sang because Deesha was alive. Then a reassuring hand reached out and touched her left shoulder. A familiar voice asked, "Are you all right?" And disappointment pulled her back to reality.

Portia read her thoughts, and said, "Sorry to disappoint."

"It's not that," said Sophia.

"I know," said her friend and lover.

Portia reached out and held Sophia's hand. As the external inferno carbonized the white skin of the capsule, the same thought went through her mind. Portia and Sophia wondered whether they would survive the landing. Moreover, each sensed that one of them would perish in the landing although which one was unclear. Each hoped that the other survived. But, as fate would have it, that was not necessarily the best thing.

For a few brief moments in the entire cosmic scheme of things, between the Big Bang and the Big Crunch, they had been alive. They had shared a place in the galaxy, in the universe, and with one another. They had been in love. And they thought, as they plummeted to Rancor, that it might soon be coming to a pathetic and regrettable end. So, Portia squeezed Sophia's hand tightly. And in that squeeze was the message: I love you ... forever. And Sophia squeezed back.

They were relieved when the incineration ended, and the deep blue of the upper atmosphere transformed to the robin's egg blue of a sunny day. The capsule caught the air, as it was designed to do, and glided. And for a few moments, they enjoyed a God's eye view of Rancor. They seemed to hang in the air without moving, the slow approach of the ground becoming incrementally more rapid with each passing tick of the clock. They passed into a layer of thick clouds. And when they came out below, the atmosphere was dark, dismal, and foreboding. The parachutes deployed but wrapped around themselves and failed to open. And the ground came up to meet them altogether too fast.

It was not a good landing. They hit the ground fast and harder than Sophia would have thought it possible to experience and survive. They bounced a dozen times before the capsule came to rest. And there were casualties.

Everything that was loose crashed to the floor.

Portia was in the midst of blowing Sophia a kiss when the ground rushed up. She was turned in her seat with her neck twisted to look over her right shoulder when the first impact occurred. And Portia's long, thin neck unexpectedly snapped like a twig. With every bounce that the capsule made after that, her head flipped back and forth like a marionette whose strings had been clipped. One real moment she was there, alive and vibrant. The next surreal moment, she was gone. She was dead. And that was that.

Sophia and three members of her team who were bruised and shaken but nonetheless intact helped get everyone outside the small craft. Only then did they tally the cost in human lives. Daphne had been spaced during the missile attack. Lydia was missing and presumed killed in the attack, as well. Portia broke her neck during the crash landing. Rhode's back was broken. Thana was blind. And Zosime had two broken legs, was bleeding internally, and unlike her name was not expected to survive. None of them were. That left Agatha, Cassandra, Gia, and herself to see to the others.

The surviving members of the Gabrielican crew were disoriented, frightened, and full of regrets about traveling so far just to have their journey end in such a manner. And they were angry.

"Maybe we can reason with them," said Agatha.

"Does this look like the handiwork of a civilization dominated by reason?" asked Gia.

"Chances are," said Cassandra to Sophia, "none of us will survive the night. They, no doubt, know where we came down. Those who are mobile have to get out of here as soon as possible. They'll be looking for us. Those who are injured will have to be left behind, and hope for the best. Hostile Scenario Protocol is in effect."

"Agreed,' said Sophia

The others nodded.

"Travelers get a med kit and emergency provisions," said Sophia. "Gia, Agatha, see to it."

"Done and done," said Gia. She and Agatha rushed back into the smoldering capsule to retrieve emergency provisions for the four of them.

Sophia spoke to the Gabrielican Sisters of Atonement that she was forced to leave behind. "I am sorry for everything," she said to start with. "I recruited each and every one of you. And look what has become of us right from the get go. I filled your heads with concepts like duty, honor, and sacrifice. But I never imagined this. In my wildest imagination, I never saw this coming. And I beg forgiveness. It was my duty to watch over you, and to protect you. And I have failed you. Now, it is my duty to survive."

Cassandra initiated the emergency beacon, which emitted a repeating set of telemetric screeches that surged up through the atmosphere to the orbiting buoy launched earlier. Their location, names, and situation was embedded within the telemetry as was a warning to all sentient travelers to make no landing there, that Rancor was hostile. Then Cassandra initiated timed self-destruction of the capsule so Tellusian technology would not fall into alien hands.

Supplies were distributed. Hugs and kisses were exchanged.

"Mother," said Cassandra, "vehicles approach. It's time to go."

"Go," said Sophia. "The three of you ... go."

89

And Agatha, Gia, and Cassandra took off to the east, to the south, and to the west respectively.

"If you want," said Sophia to the injured members of her crew, "I will stay with you, my children, until the very end, come what may."

"Go, Sophia," said Rhode, through her 3-Methyl Morphine stupor, from where she was stretched out on the ground with her broken back.

"Go, Mother," cried Thana, from where she sat with her burned eyes wrapped in gauze. "There is little time left."

"Go," pleaded Zosime the pure, who refused to take narcotics to battle the grinding pain of shattered femurs, "and God be with you."

"And also with you," whispered Sophia. Then she added, "God be with you all."

Sophia ran frantically to the north over the flat landscape of the alien world away from her crashed capsule and her dead and wounded sisters. She ran instinctively for cover in a realm that had no cover. She ran in fear of the creatures that had knocked her descending starship out of the sky.

Every instinct told Sophia to run for her life. She had sensed that something was desperately wrong, that she and her sisters had been deceived; that the Rancorians had lied to them the instant that Deesha received instructions to land in the desert. It was far from any major Rancorian city. It was in the middle of nowhere. And it just didn't seem right. Now that she and the Gabrielicans were on Rancor itself, the Rancorians could be seen for what they truly were. And their actions spoke volumes. Sophia saw now that the Rancorians were deceptive and evil masquerading as good.

"Good liars," she said to herself, as she reached an uplift of arkose sedimentation jutting up from the desert floor. She took a sip of water and thought about Deesha. Violet of God had approached the planet honestly and openly with shields down to show the Rancorians that she and the Tellusians came in peace. And, because of her naivety, the sophisticated sentient starship succumbed to a primitive missile, was damaged, and fell from the sky. She came down fast and hard thirty miles downrange from the capsule. In her mind's eye, Sophia could see Deesha burned, crumpled, and ruined. But she refused to imagine her as dead. She saw her as damaged, hurt, and holed up. She saw her as repairing herself or hoped she was.

Rancorian troops arrived by ground vehicle shortly after, and cordoned off the area. Air ships of an unknown design flew overhead.

90

As Sophia stared, she saw flashes of light coming from the crash site. Several seconds later, the staccato pops of primitive projectile weapons fire reached her. And she knew that the Gabrielicans she left behind were dead. What kind of people would kill nuns?

Sophia kissed her fingertips and made a cross in the air over the image of the crash site and her deceased Gabrielicans. And she said, "May the Lord pardon thee whatever sins or faults thou hast committed." Then she closed her eyes, and said a small prayer for them. "Mother, Father, Sister, Brother," she prayed. "Bless and keep my precious friends who died here today. Hold them close to your bosoms and love them. They died before they had the chance to spread the Word of the Mother through the *Book of Gabriel*. But that was their intention. They were good girls, all of them, and would have made good Angels. I offer this prayer in the name of the Trinity, and in the name of the Goddess of Tellus Mater. Amen."

Sophia was determined to bury the bodies of her departed sisters once the Rancorians departed. But when she saw the corpses piled, like so much firewood, aboard a Rancorian land vehicle and taken away, she realized that it was not meant to be. Their bodies were destined for chemical and microscopic analysis, dissection, and preservation in large plastic vats filled with formaldehyde in some top secret storage facility. They would never again see the light of day. And they would never rest in peace.

Chapter 15 - deceivers

Sophia and her three surviving sisters took off to the four corners of the wind from the crash site. All were pregnant. All had been filled with anticipation, expectation, and exuberance about landing, living, and ministering on the new world. But those bubbles were now burst. The ugly truth was that the Rancorians had lied to them for years. They were not the genuine article. They were deceivers.

The Rancorians fired missiles at Utera Lysanderos and knocked the living, organic starship from the sky high in the atmosphere. Two of the Gabrielicans perished in the attack. Deesha, separated from the Tellusians, alone and injured, landed roughly. Four of the Gabrielicans were injured when the capsule parachutes failed to unfurl properly and it crashed. The Rancorians killed them and took them away for biological examination and specimen storage. And now, the four Tellusians who survived the unwarranted aerial assault, the rough landing, and the murders were running for their lives. They were chased by government trained sociopaths who thought it good sport to lure aliens to their planet, hunt them, catch them, break them physically and psychologically, then crucify them.

Sophia hid within a crack in the large rock and watched the capsule self-destruct. She saw six Rancorian soldiers fall over presumably killed by shrapnel from the blast. And she was glad. God knows how many officers were inside, gloating at the advanced alien technology that had fallen into their laps, when the countdown reached zero. In a flash conflagration of light and heat fueled by pure oxygen, the white interior of the capsule and everyone inside was turned to blackened toast. And that was that.

Sophia shut her eyes and listened to the sizzling of the Tellusian capsule, as it burned. And she wondered whether Deesha, somewhere downrange, had initiated self-immolation herself rather than give up her secrets to the hostile aliens. She wondered whether Violet of God was even alive. And, as if in answer to a prayer, she heard her.

"Help me," Deesha screamed in Sophia's mind. She had lit herself ablaze yet was afraid to die. "Help me, Father," the Utera screeched with such intensity that blood sprayed out of Sophia's eyes and upon the red granite upon which her face was pressed. "I am scared," she cried out into the galaxy, hoping to hear the soothing voices of her sister Utera in her time of need. But the highly ionized Rancorian atmosphere reduced her telepathic shrieks to barely noticeable whispers lost amid the background noise of the spiral galaxy.

"Do not despair," said Sophia to her Utera and friend, in a telepathic voice that was calm like cool water amid her own distress. "Do not destroy yourself."

"Sophia. Is that you?"

"It's me, old friend," said Sophia.

"You live, still?"

"So it would seem," said Sophia, "and so must you, Deesha. Put out your fires. Repair yourself. Defend yourself. You are our only hope to escape this Hell."

The Rancorians found Utera Lysanderos shortly after and attempted to board her. But they could not find an entry portal. So, they relocated her, stored her, and attempted to examine her interior by other means. But Utera Lysanderos shielded herself so that the Rancorian x-rays and radar would not penetrate. All that the radiation did was feed her and help her with repairs while she waited for Sophia and the others to return. Violet of God longed for the time when she could once again feel the soft touch upon her skin of creatures who loved her.

The Rancorians discovered Sophia a week later amid the derelicts of society who existed in the desert. The derelicts took her in when she needed their help. She, in turn, ministered to them. They embraced her as a friend. And they adopted her teachings from the *Book of Gabriel* about love and God. But amid the group of drug addicts, drunks, and discarded social misfits was a disguised agent of the state who reported her to the authorities. And they arrived shortly after she began to preach the Word.

"She's the one you want," the agent pointed.

"You have done a good job," said the officer in charge. "Arrest her," he ordered, and his men seized Sophia. "Come," the officer said to the agent, "ride with me." And the government agent, a Judas now among the misfits, left the group, his true colors revealed and his cover blown, to join the officer in the back of his limousine.

The Rancorian authorities subdued Sophia by shocking her. They shot darts into her and shocked her with fifty thousand volt pulses that forced her muscles into tetany and drove her to the ground. They shackled her ankles and handcuffed her wrists, loaded her aboard an unmarked truck, and transported her from her ministry among the derelict Rancorian refuse to a secret military base.

The Rancorian military on special assignment rounded up the derelicts too, and transported them to a processing plant where the recent converts to Gabriel were dumped into a large melting pot of enzymes and were disintegrated. They were dangerous and had to be exterminated before the teachings that Sophia instilled in their minds was allowed to spread. To the authoritarian leaders of Rancor, Sophia's teachings about love, forgiveness, and God were blasphemous. They went against everything Rancor stood for. If those ideas were allowed to circulate amid the general population, the authorities would lose the tight control they had over the lives of the people, and anarchy would ensue. So the authorities saw to it that all Tellusian contamination was excised.

As for Sophia, first they examined her. Then they tortured her. Then they crucified her. It was the Rancorian Rule of Three.

At the outset, the physical examination was noninvasive. She was forced to strip naked, and while she stood there, they made notes about her physical appearance and dimensions, and took photographs. They took her blood pressure and recorded her heart beat and rate. They swabbed some epithelial cells from the inside of her right cheek and analyzed her DNA. They placed her on a sliding stage and rolled her into a large doughnut that slammed her with radiation and took detailed image slices of her entire body. In a few minutes the apparently noninvasive test exposed her to more radiation than she had been exposed to in her entire life. The slices were assembled into a three dimensional computer representation. Based on that representation and on comparative biology, the Rancorian scientists guessed at what her organs were and did.

Tellusian Seed by Mark Carter

When the invasive medical procedures began, Sophia was
unprepared. She had never been pricked, probed, or prodded in her
life. But now, here it was all at once. It was insulting. It was an
invasion of her personal space tantamount to rape. And it was painful.
The Rancorian doctors took blood from her right arm with a small bore
needle. That wasn't so bad. Then they stuck a large bore four inch
needle into her right knee and extracted synovial fluid. The puncture
was so painful that Sophia wanted to knock the head off the doctor
performing the procedure. But she was afraid that the needle would
move if she did, and would damage her knee more.

The Rancorians placed her on an operating table after that, turned
her on her side, and strapped her down. They inserted a black, flexible
pipe into her mouth, and pushed it down her throat, and into her
stomach. The light at the end of the pipe illuminated her interior with
light so intense that her upper abdomen could be seen glowing orange
and yellow from the outside. A similar but larger and longer pipe was
pushed up her anus to navigate her large bowel. The pipes had pincers
on the ends to take tissue samples. And the doctors did so at the push
of a button. Snap. Snap. Snap. But those probings were not as painful
as the biopsies that were to come.

They bored a chunk of flesh from her right buttocks. They cut into
her chest wall and bored a sample of heart and lung. They cut into her
abdomen and bored a sample of liver, spleen, pancreas, kidney, and
adrenal gland. They cut into her throat and bored a sample of her
thyroid. Then they unclasped her, forced her to a sitting position,
screwed a metal halo onto her head, shaved the fiery-orange hair from
her right temporal region, drilled a hole through her skull, and biopsied
her brain.

The Rancorian doctors performed all of their painful procedures on
Sophia without anesthetic or sedation. To them, she was an organism.
And they had no regard for her discomfort. By training, they were
detached and distant from the organism. They were purists. The only
things important to them were the numbers, and where those numbers
fell amid the given parameters.

When the so-called medical tests were over, Sophia was dumped
naked in a prison cell. She was bloodied, bruised, in shock, and utterly
traumatized. But the Rancorian authorities had what they wanted.
They knew her physical limits. They knew how hard she could be
pushed. And they knew how easily she could be killed. The Tellusians

were not as advanced as they suggested. They could be killed just as easily as the next alien. The Rancorians knew everything necessary to begin the next phase in her examination. It was called information extraction.

They kept Sophia naked and unwashed for days, in the way Rancorians count days, and subjected her to loud bells and horns to keep her awake. They knew that everyone broke if deprived of the essentials for long enough. So they refused her water when she was thirsty, food when she was hungry, and sleep when she was tired. They worked in teams to break her. And in the end, they won.

"Why are you here?"

"We came to spread the Word of God."

"God does not exist."

"We only exist because of God."

"God only exists because of you."

A fresh team worked her over every twenty minutes. They questioned her and they accused her.

"It is obvious that you are a spy."

"I am not a spy."

"It says so right here on this document. You are accused of espionage. So, you are a spy."

"I am a missionary."

"So, you admit that you are on a mission."

"We are here to spread the Word of God."

"That is blasphemy. God does not exist. What is your real mission?"

"We are here to preach the *Book of Gabriel*."

"Books are forbidden. Preaching is forbidden."

The teams changed once again. This team brought in large cards, the kind sometimes used on kindergarteners to help the children associate words with objects.

They showed her a red card, and asked, "What is this color?"

"Red."

They showed her a green card, and asked, "What is this color?"

"It is Green."

They pointed upward, and asked, "What is this direction?"

"Up."

They pointed downward, and asked, "What is this direction?"

And she said, "Down."

Within five days, red was green, up was down, and she admitted to being a spy. By her own confession, she was an enemy of the state sent to undermine the Rancorian government with subversive ideas about forgiveness, love, and God. She would have done anything, said anything, and did, just to have food, water, and sleep. Once she buckled, she was given water and a modest meal. They allowed her to have a shower. They gave her simple clothes and a blanket. Then she was put back in her cell awaiting execution.

The Rancorians played a loop of Sophia's alien confession over and over on the network news. And the typical Rancorian, utterly manipulated by what he saw and heard, was convinced that she was the enemy. When it was announced that this strange alien was to be publicly executed, the typical Rancorian guzzled his beer and cheered. It was only right. It was deserved. How dare this strange creature come to his world and do such things? How dare it?

Sophia hoped that only she had been captured. She hoped that her surviving Sisters escaped the Rancorian search teams, located Utera Lysanderos, made their way to Deesha, and escaped the planet.

In the end, two things broke Sophia. What the Rancorians did to her was deep and personal. First, they ripped off her wings. Then they killed her unborn child.

"You're pregnant," the Radiologist announced when he viewed Sophia's scan. It came as no surprise to her. She underwent embryonic implantation prior to the launch of Utera Lysanderos. All of the Gabrielicans aboard a thousand starships were pregnant on that bright, spring morning when they launched. It was a precaution just in case they did not return.

"We can't have that," said the doctor, as he injected her with hormones that brought on severe cramping and miscarriage. In his cruelty, he pickled the embryo right before her eyes. And to torture her even more, he placed the bottle on the other side of a shatterproof window for her to view all day.

The stress of her torture, culminating in her miscarriage, brought about Sophia's transformation to Angel. Wings appeared on her back, extended through her chest, and melded with an organ located near her heart that the medical professionals had previously identified but had not understand. After Sophia's transformation, the organ glowed bright yellow, and her examiners and inquisitors speculated that it was an energy center.

But the physicians became frightened when the organ showed an exponential increase in energy. So they did what doctors do best. They excised it. At the outset of Sophia's change, while she was still fragile, her mental and physical torturers decided to remove the mysterious organ and to literally cut off her wings. And that was the end of her. Like a butterfly disembodied by a cruel eviscerator, she was undone. She could no longer talk with her sisters telepathically. And she could no longer converse with Deesha.

Killing her unborn child, removing her energy organ, and tearing off her wings broke Sophia's heart and soul. It was the final assault on a stalwart mind. It was the deepest cut in a series of rapes designed to utterly break her spirit. And it succeeded.

After that, she agreed with anything they proposed. If they said, "Jump up and down on one foot," she asked, "Which foot?" If they insisted that red was green, it was. And if they said she was an enemy of the state, who was she to question it? Beyond deprivation of food, sleep, and water, the rude removal of her wings was the final straw, and she succumbed entirely. She gave in to their devious and evil machinations. She gave up.

Sophia was drugged stupid and dragged bleeding and naked before three bearded men dressed in white robes and black turbans. The well attired kangaroo tribunal proclaimed her guilty before the fact of twenty-three crimes against God under Rancorian religious law. And without defense, because it was not permitted, she was sentenced to death by crucifixion three times over for good measure. For a lesser crime, she would have been sentenced to death by stoning three times over in a tradition similar to that found on Earth of long ago among countries ruled by similarly misogynistic religious sects.

Sophia's execution was televised for the world to watch. Only the most notorious religious criminals were executed in such a manner. The Rancorian government televised an execution when they wanted to make a point. It was a politically and religiously motivated spectacle. And the point they wanted to make was that unideas, ideas that were not approved by the state religion, alien ideas, were dangerous and would not be tolerated. The government did not even mention the ideas that Sophia was accused of spreading. The mere mention of them might lead to a plague of madness and to religious anarchy, and order had to be maintained.

More to the point, Sophia frightened the men of Rancor. She made them feel inadequate. She made them feel insecure. She made them feel like little boys. And so, the men did what little boys do when confronted with a woman who arouses them sexually and intimidates them intellectually. They destroyed her. They broke her physically and psychologically. They accused her of crimes she did not commit. And they rubber stamped her for crucifixion because their male dominated, profit-oriented religion allowed such barbaric sadism in the name of God. In the opinion of Rancorian clerics, women were filthy and not to be trusted, at the best of times, and were granted few rights. Alien women had no rights whatever.

Chapter 16 - hephzibah

Since wood no longer existed, Sophia was hung like a piece of meat onto a cross made of plastic in the middle of the great Rancorian desert amid oil derricks and pumps. And to her great dismay, two of her Gabrielican sisters were already hanging there, crucified just like her. Agatha was already dead. But Gia was still alive. When their eyes met, they wept for the plight of the other. Each had hoped that the other had gotten away. But alas, it was not to be.

Sophia sighed, and then asked, "What has become of Cassandra?"

"I have not seen her," said Gia.

"Perhaps," said Sophia.

"Yes, my darling sister, perhaps."

"Father, Mother, Sister, Brother," Sophia prayed quietly, in the old manner, to God Almighty, the Virgin, Hephzibah, and Christ all at once, and all as one, with her face pressed against the cross. "Help me. Help us. Please help us. Deliver us from this evil. Please God, deliver us from this pain."

But the pain of her crucified flesh spiked with the slightest movement. Muscles cramped in tetany cried out for relaxation. Skin burned crisp by the severe Rancorian sun cried out for darkness. And her parched body cried out for water that the Rancorians sadistically refused.

When Sophia's pain became intolerable, she passed out for a time, which was a blessing. And she dreamed. She dreamed about the lush, green vegetation on Tellus Mater. She dreamed about floating atop the fresh water of the reservoir near her home on a hot summer day after senior graduation just before she entered the order. She dreamed of a time when her fragile flesh was perfect and pristine, and she was truly happy, if only for a moment.

But it was short-lived. As always, the monster came then. It surfaced from the depths with mouth agape and homodont teeth poised to insinuate their vicious displeasure. And when its jaw closed and crushed her, when she was unable to breathe or to scream, and when its pointy serrated teeth sliced flesh and cracked bone, and she could stand the pain no more, she awoke to the hellish agony of Rancorian crucifixion and reality.

Sophia felt the spikes penetrating the backs of her hands and feet again. It was, of course, a trick of the mind, but felt real nonetheless. And she cried out. "Help me, God. Please, God. Please, help me." But she knew that she was nothing in the scheme of things. Her pleas would most likely go unanswered because God had more important things to do than to save Gia and her from crucifixion. And her destiny, as it appeared to her in the here and now, as she hung from the brown, plastic cross in the desert of a godless and repulsive alien world, was simple. After a short life lived virtuously and dedicated to the teachings of Gabriel, her destiny was to suffer, bleed out, and die. To her, it was a test of faith. And, for the most part, she accepted it as such. Yet, at the same time, despite the obvious, despite her plight, she didn't believe that her destiny was to die there. She had always imagined something other for herself. And so, she cried out into the universe for deliverance. Perhaps, she thought, it was only a matter of time before God heard her. After all, he took his sweet time saving the Son.

Some scholars argued that God was imaginary, that he and his so-called Son were fiction, reworked mythology written as gospel. But Sophia dismissed the naysayers. They were the same cynics that saw no proof of God in the world around them. But the Gabrielican Sisters of Atonement saw with better eyes than that. They believed in Father, Mother, Sister and Brother with all of their hearts and souls. And with those better eyes that their belief bestowed, they saw evidence of God everywhere, in all of her manifestations.

So, Sophia prayed. Amid her pain and suffering, agonizing consciousness and troubled dream, she prayed for deliverance. She prayed for forgiveness. And she prayed for salvation.

Sophia's eyes rolled insanely and scanned the little piece of sky that she could see. It looked like two o'clock in the afternoon. And she laughed out loud because, under normal circumstances, it was time for her sisters and herself to have their mid-afternoon break. From a Kelly green demitasse with maroon interior and matching Kelly green saucer, she would drink steaming black espresso filled to the brim and topped with ecru froth. With it, she would have a biscotto. And for five minutes, she would swim in the small indulgence of the gustatory and olfactory Heaven on Earth that made the verisimilitudes of the day bearable. Whereas, now, while hanging on the plastic cross, all she tasted was the iron flavor of spilled blood. And all she smelled was the ammonia reek of bitter tears.

Sophia wasn't sure when she passed the point of no return. Perhaps she was beyond it before she was stripped bare, held to, and nailed to the cross. She wasn't sure. But there came a point where she no longer believed she could recover physically from the injuries that were inflicted upon her, even if she had the power to miraculously step down from the cross. Moreover, there came a point where she was so tired and so weak that she doubted, for an instant, the very existence of God. But she quickly begged God to forgive her for her weakness. And it was when she was at her most desolate that Messengers appeared.

Gia and Sophia survived three days of excruciating agony that felt like thirty. In the end, when the Gabrielican nuns could take no more, they begged Hephzibah to be merciful. And she was. The goddess of Tellus Mater heard them and saw them from her purple padded throne watching over Tellus Mater. And her heart bled for them. But she could not leave her post because she sensed that all Hell was about to break loose there, and she was needed. So, she sent three Archangels to their aid instead.

Of all the ways to die, crucifixion hit home with Hephzibah on a personal level because of her emotional experience, on Earth, with Adonai when he walked the world as Jesus of Nazareth so long ago. She couldn't stomach the sadism of crucifixion when she was Seraph. And now that she was Goddess of Tellus Mater, she would not tolerate it. As rare as that form of cruel, public execution was in the entire multiverse, when it came to her attention, she exceeded her purview and stepped in to end it. She would forever associate crucifixion with the torture of her beloved. She simply could not help it. Diana the Mother of Creation, God Almighty, and Adonai himself saw that her feelings concerning the matter were so powerful that they even transcended the painful emotional punishment that the Father inflicted upon her for usurping his authority at Golgotha. So, they came to respect her enduring passion and to support her actions as just and true.

When Hephzibah could not attend to a crucifixion directly, she sent her trusted representatives to act on her behalf and to perform miracles in her name. And so, when Gia and Sophia cried out for Hephzibah, in desperation, during the closing hours of their crucifixion in the Rancorian desert, Azrael, Raphael, and Zadkiel were seconded from Heaven and appeared behind the fragile females.

The Seraphim seconded to Hephzibah as Archangels stared at the three Gabrielican Sisters of Atonement crucified backwards and were rightly offended. The nuns were crucified facing their crosses of brown plastic not to protect their modesty, not to hide their breasts, but rather to expose their backs to the crowd. And in so doing, the Rancorians exposed the most precious part of the dedicated servants of Hephzibah to alien ridicule. The Rancorians exposed the naked flesh of the young women. Moreover, the aliens exposed the ornate oriental artwork tattooed on the backs and buttocks of the young women to the light of day. And that was simply wrong. The tattoos were symbols of their full commitment to the order. The tattoos were meant to be seen only by themselves and the Goddess. For the Rancorians to reveal the magnificent artwork was literally throwing pearls before swine. And the Archangels, who possessed tattoos of their own given to them by God, marking them as special and delineating their power, sympathized and were angered by the violation. To them, it was tantamount to rape.

Unlike the tattoos that once offended God the Mother, the Gabrielicans had received special permission from the Goddess to bear the tattoos in her honor. Like the ornate tattoos worn by the Seraphim, and, to a lesser degree, by the entire Chorus, it marked them as beautiful, individual, and unique.

The tattoos that the Gabrielicans bore took years to acquire. They were entire scenes created with the meticulous craftswomanship of an artist and mistress, herself a nun, who did exclusive work for the order. They were tattooed with love and piety for the Goddess by a woman devoted to her entirely who was herself quite blind. She tattooed her subjects by feel, by running her elderly, supersensitive fingertips over every inch of their backs, and by feeling every nuance of their quivering flesh, every hill and valley of their supple anatomy, and every blemish, freckle, and rough region of her previous work.

The mistress craftswoman tattooed entire graduating classes of nuns simultaneously a year before their convocations. And it was the highlight of every ceremony when the novitiates dropped their old garb and exposed their tattoos before all in attendance. After that, they took their final vows, and were *bone fide* Gabrielican Sisters of Atonement. They dressed in the formal habits of the order. And their tattoos were concealed forever.

When the Archangels looked at the tattooed backs of the tortured nuns, they saw evolved human beings who had made a commitment to the Goddess. They saw individuals sent out into the Milky Way to spread the Word of the Mother through the *Book of Gabriel*. They saw beauty and devotion much like their own to the Trinity. And, like their own hearts broken during the War of Heaven so long ago, they also sensed great sadness. And they were touched.

The Archangels looked upon the three crucified nuns and remembered Golgotha, Jesus Christ, and his pathetic demolition. They were there when Hephzibah cursed the Jews and the Romans, and brought a rain of meteorites down upon the middle-east. They were there and witnessed it all: God's delay, the sublime suffering of the fragile man-god, and the deific wrath of a Seraph. And so, even here in the future, in this remote location, on this desolate world, they were reminded of the sadism, and were offended.

Azrael, Raphael, and Zadkiel hovered above the oil-soaked sand of the Rancorian desert and stared at the crucified nuns with all of the love of the Goddess and with all of the love of Heaven combined. The three Archangels cried out in anguish. And the sound of their seraphic voices was as a thousand trumpets and caused everyone in attendance to drop to the ground unconscious. But Agatha did not hear the voices of the Archangels because she was dead. And what Gia and Sophia heard was the melodic whispers of Messengers because they were protected.

And Azrael, the first among them, whose name means *Who God Helps*, spoke to the nuns, even to Agatha's soul who hovered there still. He asked Agatha's lost spirit if she wished him to escort her before the throne of the Goddess because it was what he did. But she would not abandon her sisters, and said, "No." He asked Gia and Sophia if they desired for him to end their suffering, to take their souls from their devastated bodies, and to bring them before the Goddess, as well. But they also said, "No." They told him that there was much they still had left to do in this life, although their lives were quickly approaching an apparent end. They told him that they had seen it in visions. When he read their thoughts, he could see that it was so. And who was he to interfere with destiny. So, he bowed before them, and receded.

Then Raphael, the second among them, whose name means *God Heals*, asked the nuns whether they wished to be repaired. And they said, "Yes." So, Raphael ended their stigmata. He pulled them down gently from their crosses of brown plastic, and repaired their spike-stabbed hands and feet. He revived Agatha and repaired her wounds. He restored their wings and the energy centers in their chests that made them Angels. And most miraculous of all, he restored the small, fragile life that had been growing in their wombs. And once all was accomplished, he too bowed before them, and receded.

And finally, Zadkiel, the third among them, whose name means the *Righteousness of God*, asked the three Gabrielican nuns, as they stood there naked and vulnerable, and filled with hatred toward their Rancorian interrogators and torturers, to forgive their oppressors. And it was hard. But they tried. And when they finally calmed their hearts and did, he shone his benevolence and mercy upon them because it was what he did. And he removed the trauma of their misadventure from their minds and souls.

The Archangels cleansed the stained bodies of the crucified nuns, clothed them in fresh habits, and placed new sandals upon their feet. And when all was said and done, the Seraphs transported the fledgling Angels back to Tellus Mater, at the speed of deific thought.

Azrael, Raphael, and Zadkiel delivered Agatha, Gia, and Sophia into the waiting arms of the Goddess. And Hephzibah showered kisses upon the Tellusians for being faithful and steadfast in the face of great adversity. And so, the First Daughter of Heaven placed the one-time Gabrielicans, since they were more than that now, in her *sanctum sanctorum* where they would remain until a new God arose, Tellus Mater became the center of the seventh universe, and the services of three nascent Angels would be needed.

When the Rancorians returned to consciousness, the Tellusian missionaries were gone, seemingly snatched from their crosses of brown plastic by forces unseen. So, to conceal the unexplainable, the guards charged with overseeing the sadistic spectacle sprayed the crosses with liquefied petrochemical distillates and set them ablaze, as they had planned to do all along. And the synthetic crosses burned hot, filled the sky with noxious, black smoke, and melted into brittle, deformed globs.

Chapter 16 - hephzibah

Records of the Tellusian landing on Rancor were excised. Tapes were burned. Witnesses were sworn to secrecy. Some were eliminated. And the story about the crash in the desert, the alien autopsies, the surreal crucifixions and vanishings, the Tellusian known as Cassandra who was never caught, and the living starship Utera Lysanderos that went missing quickly faded into the unsubstantiated obscurity of folk lore and legend, and was eventually forgotten altogether.

Chapter 17 - regret

Abraxas sat upon his throne within the golden-domed Citadel in the heart of Heaven and imagined himself standing in the stillness of the Mandala Room amid the dim glow of trillions of galaxies spread over the eight arms of the multiverse shaped like a starfish. He came to the Mandala Room in his imagination each deific day to celebrate the progress of his creations and to lament the demise of his failures. He had so many regrets. He had so many tears.

Hephaestia had been right when she accused him of being imperfect so long ago. He was. The Mother of Creation knew it but loved him unconditionally. The entire Chorus realized he was flawed, was human in a sense, although he was far from a human being. But even with his flaws, compared to them, compared to the Seraphim, Cherubim, Archangels and Angels, he was perfection or as near to perfection as God could be except the Mother who was truly perfect.

Abraxas cried especially for the most precious of his failures. He cried for Adam and for Eve. He cried for Earth and all of his creations that lived and died upon the small water world. He was angry at himself, at his absolutism. He should have been more understanding. He should have been more flexible. He should have been more forgiving.

Abraxas caught himself indulging in self-pity. And he pulled back.

"Could have, should have, would have," he said aloud, as he swept his right hand before his face and dismissed his thoughts. And like tears in rain, his regret washed away.

Elektra of the Seraphim, and third Princess of Heaven, stood before the fiery throne of God the Father with head bowed in veneration.

"You have summoned me," stated Elektra, "and I am here to serve you."

God Almighty opened his eyes and looked upon the miniscule Daughter of Paradise standing before him.

"Open your eyes and look upon me, child," he said.

Elektra raised her eyes and looked upon God, as only a few creatures in all of creation are allowed. Even though, to look upon him was like staring into the sun.

"Yes, Father," she whispered.

"Soon," he said, "the Mother of Creation will divest your sister Hephzibah from her duties as Goddess of Tellus Mater because she stands in the way of destiny. Hephzibah will be reassigned. Meanwhile, the females of Tellus shall be lost to us, except one, swept up in the vicissitudes of the cruel mistress. Her name is Ariel, and she is of utmost importance. I assign you, my daughter, to watch over her for she is on the verge of becoming."

Elektra stared at God Almighty and considered the give and take of his Manichean words. Then she asked, "Becoming what, Father?"

The Father was taken aback by the question. He assumed that Elektra knew.

"God," said God, "of a kind."

Now it was Elektra's turn to be surprised.

"She will be the first human being to achieve what I planted in the DNA of her ancestors long ago," said God, "and evolve into god. She will not be like your Mother, or me, or the Son. But she will be a child god of a new kind, and endowed with great power. Do you understand?"

"I am trying to comprehend," said Elektra. "But I have never, in all of creation, witnessed any creature on the brink of becoming."

"Verily, I say unto you," said the Father, "she is the first of her kind in the entire multiverse. But she may not be the last. She is the inevitable result of evolution amid the cold matter that I seeded across the multiverse shaped like a starfish in the Mandala Room of Heaven. She shall become god of a kind, and shall rise up above the colored sand of her universe bathed in perpetual darkness, protected and still, and hold dominion over billions of glowing galaxies containing billions of stars and the cornucopia of life that they support."

Elektra furled her brow and raised her right index finger looking very much like a Russian iconic painting. God nodded.

"To go back, Father," she said. "What of the planet? What of the inhabitants of Tellus Mater? There are tens of millions of them. My task is to watch over Ariel, but what of the others?"

"Nothing," said God.

"Nothing," cried Elektra. "Oh, Father, nothing?"

"They are not your concern," he said. "Neither shall they be Hephzibah's concern once the Mother has spoken with her. The Daughters of Tellus Mater have served their function as the final step in human evolution leading to Ariel. What she shall evolve into will no longer be human. The sacrifice of the Daughters is the cost that humans must pay so that one of them, the Ariel of which I speak, may become god."

"The price is too high," wept Elektra.

"I know," said God Almighty, as he stroked her hair. "I know. Breathe my daughter. Calm yourself, my fiery Angel. And see what I see."

In her seraphic mind, Elektra saw what was to come to the small water world. She saw the invading star ships. She witnessed their vicious attack. She, Hephzibah, Thea, or Arabella could have averted the unprovoked assault easily. And, without God's intervention, they would have done so naturally because it was in their nature to be protective. But without the nuclear attack and the radiation that it released into the environment of Tellus Mater, the child she was tasked to watch over would never transform. The young, evolved, human female would remain latent, forever the caterpillar and never the butterfly. She would never metamorphose from Homo angelicus to Theo. She would never become god. And human destiny would never be fulfilled.

Chapter 18 - tempest

Athena and the Gabrielican novitiates were delivered, by Xuxa, to the habitable zone of the Milky Way, within the rarefied supernova remnant of Geminga, in the Gould Belt, near the inner rim of the Orion Arm, to the Sol System, to the planet Tellus Mater, and to the equivalent of an Iowa cornfield in late summer during the extreme heat of late afternoon just before a thunderstorm.

"I sense," said Xuxa, "that I have brought you to the right place but ahead of time, as human beings calculate time. You seek a young Tellusian farm girl named Ariel. Befriend her. See to it that no harm befalls her. In time, you shall be joined by the Third Daughter of Paradise sent by Almighty God. And together you and she shall bear witness to this child's becoming."

"How do you know these things?" asked Athena.

"I just know," said Xuxa. "Here. You will need this."

Xuxa handed Athena a small leather purse that jingled with coins.

"What's this?"

"Gold," said Xuxa. "You will need it. Spend it wisely."

Athena quickly tucked the purse into the deep, right pocket of her habit.

The friends hugged, kissed, and said their heartfelt good-byes. They wished each other good luck. And when all was said and done, Xuxa stepped away from Athena, gazed at the dark clouds, and said, "Make haste. A storm approaches. She who you seek shall be found in a cellar." Then the Angel stepped into the ether and was gone on her journey to Heaven.

The raspy whine of cicadas on a hot summer day filled the void left by Xuxa. Athena looked at the two novitiates. They were stupid and young, and clueless about what to do next. They looked to her, as

Mother Superior, to think for them. So, the twenty-eight year old spun around before the two sixteen year olds in search of an answer.

Athena found her answer to the northwest. She spotted the hip-and-valley roof of the local farm house mounted with copper lightning rods and a brass rooster weather vane.

"God damn, it's hot," she said, as she marched along a furrow of rich, red loam toward the house. She ripped off her white Cornette and grasped it in her left hand while she ran the fingers of her right hand through her thick matt of cropped blonde hair. Her head was soaked. "Oh, that's better."

The novitiates stood where they had been delivered with mouths agape.

"She swore," said Akakallis, whose name meant daffodil.

"She took the Lord's name in vain," said Akantha, whose name meant thorn.

"If you don't move your lily white asses, Daffodil and Thorn in my side," shouted Athena, without looking back, "I will leave you behind. I swear. Come on."

The novitiates stared at each other.

"Yes, Mother Superior," said Akakallis.

"Yes, Mother," said Akantha.

Daffodil and Thorn gathered the black dress and black underskirts of their Holy Habits, at the front, exposing their functional black shoes and a bit of lower leg, picked up their small black handbags, and scrambled along the furrow, like clumsy puppies, to keep up.

"Do you understand, Ariel?" her mother asked the eleven year old, as they sat before the flickering lantern light.

Ariel thought hard about the quotation from the *Book of Gabriel*. But its meaning was beyond her. She shook her head.

"Look at the picture, then," said her mother, as she directed the child's attention to the reprint in the book before her of a much larger oil painting. She tapped on the picture with the nail of her right index finger. "Describe the picture."

Ariel crinkled her face and delved deep for an answer. "I see a woman walking over a bad road," she said.

"That's right," encouraged her mother. "What else?"

"I see the Goddess at the end of the road. She looks pretty. Doesn't she, mamma?"

"Yes, she does, my darling. What will the Goddess do to the woman when she reaches the end of the road?"

"She will hug her."

"That's right, like I hug you every day. Hugging is good."

Ariel nodded in agreement.

"And where will the Goddess take the woman?" her mother asked.

"She will take her to Heaven."

"That's right, my darling. So, let's look back at the road. You said it was a bad road. What makes it a bad road?"

"It has stones all over it, and holes," said Ariel. "It would be very difficult to walk on."

"That's right," said her mother. "Might the stones make her stumble?"

"Yes."

"Might the holes make her trip, and maybe give her a sprained ankle?"

Ariel looked at her bruised right foot with greenish body and dark blue toes from the sprain she had suffered a week before.

"Yes," she said.

"So, why does the woman keep walking on the road?"

"To get to the Goddess," said Ariel.

"That's right. So, if the woman wants to walk to the Goddess for her hug, she has to walk along that bad road."

"Yes."

"Look back at the quotation," said Ariel's mother.

A rocky road leads to God.

"Do you understand now, my Ariel?"

"Yes, mamma," said the eleven year old. "It means that the road to God is not easy."

"Yes," said her mother. "But it also means that the road to becoming God is not easy."

Ariel cocked her head like a confused puppy. She had never, in all of her eleven years, considered the possibility that she might, that any of her sisters, her kind, might become gods.

"Do you know of anyone who has become a god?" asked the child.

"We are Homo angelicus," said her mother, "the first human beings to take the evolutionary leap toward the ethereal. But none of us has

115

taken the next step. None of us has gone further, not yet. Does that disappoint you?"

"No," said Ariel. "It gives me hope. What must I do to become a god, mamma?"

"None of us knows for certain," said her mother, as she ran her thin digits through Ariel's fiery-orange hair. "But the *Book of Gabriel* suggests that we live a good life, think of others more than ourselves, believe in God because he believes in us above the highest Angels, and just be."

"Perhaps it will be you," said Ariel.

Her mother laughed. "Or perhaps, my darling," she said, "it will be you."

The nuns walked quickly along the furrow toward the farmhouse, as the weather conditions deteriorated. A black cumulonimbus cloud loomed low overhead, turning the day darker than an eclipse. Rain was in the air. Athena could smell it blowing in ahead of the storm. She picked up her pace. She did not want to be caught in the field when it turned into a lake of mud.

"I'm scared," said Daffodil.

"I'm scared, too," said Thorn.

Cold rain came first, big drops that hit the dusty soil and exploded. Heavy rain came next. Sheets of rain followed. And the novitiates squealed like piglets as they ran after Athena.

The Gabrielican nuns were soaked to the bone by the time they cleared the corn field and stepped out into the central farmyard. To the east, there was a barn, a poultry house, and a vegetable garden. To the west there was a cowshed and greenhouses. And directly in front of them, on the other side of the farmyard, was a two storey farmhouse.

"Let's go," said the Mother Superior.

Athena ran past a tractor hooked up to a pickup automatic baler parked on the edge of the yard. She ran past pickup loader, rotary hoe, and manure spreader. And she ran past a combine ready and waiting to bring in the harvest. She ran to the farmhouse and three quarters of the way around it before she stopped.

Daffodil and Thorn reached the house and ran up onto the porch that ran around the perimeter of the first floor. When Athena didn't join them, Thorn asked, "Mother, are we not going inside?" And they were shocked by her answer.

"Most assuredly not," she said. "Get down here and help me lift this door."

The Mother Superior stood in front of the slanted, steel door of a storm cellar just as the sky turned green and the sinister cloud released hail. She turned a primitive latch and unlocked the door. And the three of them opened the heavy door together.

"Watch your step," said Athena, as the novitiates stumbled down the concrete steps into the dark. Then she pulled the door shut and latched it behind them.

Hail pelted the steel door with small pings, at first, then with large bangs. And Athena knew that, had they still been outside, it would have been the equivalent of being stoned. It would have been the end of them. "Thank you, Lord," she prayed.

"I hear a voice," said Daffodil. And indeed, the Gabrielicans listened and heard a voice on a radio.

"A tornado warning has been issued for the following counties: Greene, Boone, and Story. A tornado is on the ground or eminent. If you live in these areas, you are advised to seek shelter immediately. Repeat. A tornado warning has been issued for Greene, Boone, and Story counties. A tornado has been spotted on the ground in Greene County heading northeast toward Boone and Story counties. It is accompanied by torrential rain and large hail. Seek shelter underground or in the lowest part of your house immediately. Warning …"

Ariel and her mother jumped when the inner door of their storm shelter burst open suddenly and the faces of three nuns appeared in the flickering lantern light like Halloween trick-or-treaters.

"Sorry," said Athena. "We seem to have been caught in a storm. May we join you?"

"Please, sister," said the farm woman. "You honor us with your presence."

"Mother Superior," corrected Daffodil.

"Akakallis," scolded Athena. "That was rude. Apologize."

"I beg forgiveness for my rudeness, madam," said the novitiate.

"It is I who am sorry," said the woman. "I didn't recognize your station."

"How could you?" said the Mother superior, as she sat on a plank bench bolted to the far wall of poured concrete. "It's dark. We're drenched. We don't exactly wear yellow chevrons on our habits indicating our rank. My habit smells like dog piss for which I must apologize considering these cramped quarters. And considering our situation, as your guests, I think it's inappropriate. Are you picking up on all of this, Akakallis?"

"Yes, Mother."

"So please," said the Mother Superior to the farm woman, "call me Athena."

"Helen," said the farm woman, "and this is my daughter Ariel."

Athena smiled because she had found the child just as Xuxa said.

"Ariel," said Athena. "What a beautiful name. Are you scared, Ariel?" asked Athena.

"Yes," said the child.

"Don't be," said Athena. "We have been sent by an Angel to watch over you."

Then the inner door slammed shut and rattled violently. Everyone's ears popped. The novitiates and the woman fell asleep because of the extremely low air pressure. Ariel and Athena yawned uncontrollably. And a throbbing meat grinder churned past above them.

The storm was over by morning. The severe thunderstorm and tornado warnings were cancelled. The steel door of the storm shelter was thrown back. And five exhausted survivors exited the reinforced hole in the ground and sucked in the fresh air.

Damage from the F1 funnel cloud that touched down on the farm was apparent. Equipment in the farmyard, which had been parked neatly around the perimeter, had been picked up and tossed like cardboard match boxes. The electrical poles running beside the farm road from the highway were down in a string. And the barn had been ripped to smithereens. Otherwise, most of the farm, and the farm house, in particular, had been spared.

Coffee was made. Helen cooked ham and eggs with buttered toast for everyone. And while Ariel played outside with Daffodil and Thorn, her mother and the Mother Superior discussed why the Gabrielicans were there. And Ariel's mother, being a devout woman, took Athena at her word. She expressed concerns about being able to pay for the storm damage let alone feed the extra mouths, since times were tight. But Athena placed the bag of gold coins on the table, and said, "We expect to earn our room and board. And we have been given this to cover extras. What is ours is yours."

And a deal was struck. The Gabrielicans were given permission to live and to work on the farm while they watched over Ariel. They would be her coworkers and her guardians. They would be her teachers. And when the time came, they would be there to attest to her transformation.

Chapter 19 - destiny

When the Daughters of Tellus Mater dreamed, they dreamed God's dream. It wasn't the dreams of God the Father or of God the Mother. Their deific sleeping thoughts were beyond the comprehension of the Daughters. The Tellusians dreamed about a farm on the Tuscan hills of Heaven, in springtime, about flowering grapevines, and about green fields of winter wheat. They dreamed about sunny, blue skies dotted with white clouds and about rainy nights with fresh air kissed by lightning blowing the sheers of their bedroom windows. They dreamed about pregnant Angels working the fields of Heaven. And they dreamed about themselves, in their long, denim dresses and white, linen bonnets, working the farms of Tellus Mater.

When they slept after a long day in the fields, or in the kitchens cooking for the others, they fell asleep instantly. They dreamed God's dream throughout the night, and it brought them calm and order. And when they awoke long before the dawn to start their chores, they were physically refreshed and mentally at peace with themselves, with their lives, and with their common destiny.

The Daughters awoke each morning and sang a song of joy to the Goddess, to the deity who watched over them and protected them from all things, to Hephzibah the Goddess of Tellus Mater. They sang the mantra from the *Book of Gabriel*: "Just BEEE." And they quoted his philosophy displayed under glass in needlepoint on the wall above the headboard of every bed.

Happiness is keeping busy.

And so, they began each new day.

But three days before Ariel's sixteenth birthday, the Daughters of Tellus Mater awoke askew. Their usually placid dreams had devolved into dangerous visions of death and destruction. And they awoke horrified.

Hephzibah sat on her purple, padded throne with carved golden wings licking upward like fire on each side of the backrest, and dozed off for the first time in ten thousand years. And while she slept, she dreamed about the War of Heaven that once was, and about the War of Tellus Mater that was to come. She awoke with a start to the cries of millions of Tellusians, to the voices of her Daughters praying to her, begging her to explain the dangerous visions she had transmitted to them. And she was beside herself with emotion.

"What is this thing that we have seen?" cried the voices.

"Help us, Goddess," they pleaded.

Hephzibah removed the high crown she wore shaped like three pastel blue and pink tulip petals from her fiery-orange hair, and placed it upon a golden stand beside her throne. She rolled down and removed the elegant, long, white gloves reminiscent of silk but woven from the fabric of pure energy from her arms, and draped them over the right arm rest of her throne. She rose to her feet in her long, silk gown of pastel blue, green and purple feathers with a bodice of pastel pink, and sighed. And Heaven sighed with her because she had failed the Daughters of Tellus Mater.

Hephzibah had been chosen by Flora the Goddess of Everything to protect the Daughters of Tellus Mater so they could evolve from corporeal to ethereal over time. But, while she slept, a space armada had journeyed between the stars and had taken up station keeping above the New Earth. Their starships hung over the Tellusian cities like so many swords of Damocles. Their mission was to obliterate the Tellusian philosophy by laying waste to Tellusian civilization. "Just BEEE," to them, were two of the most dangerous words in the Milky Way galaxy.

What the Daughters saw in their nightmares was the bombardment of their beautiful world from space with twenty megaton city killers. They saw their beautiful cities incinerated, in an instant, in the ten million degree heat of thermonuclear conflagration. And, for the first time in their lives, for the first time in ten thousand years, they were terrified.

Tears poured like Angel Falls down Hephzibah's deific cheeks at the vision of a world reborn destroyed once again at the hands of evil.

"Protect us, Goddess," they cried.

"Forgive us for our sins," they lamented.

But there was nothing to forgive. The Tellusians were a good people in the eyes of the Goddess. They were on an ethereal evolutionary path. One of them, in particular, was destined to become god of a kind. And the rest, those who survived the nuclear conflagration, were destined to couple with an alien species and to create a race of Angels.

Hephzibah sighed because she was helpless to save the Tellusians from destruction. In her dream she saw her right hand held back by the Mother while calamity befell the Daughters. She could protect them with a thought. She could utterly destroy the invading aliens and their home world with a blink. But she knew that the Mother would intercede. The Mother, as she had in the past, would request that Hephzibah do nothing, and let destiny take its course. And doing nothing, where the Daughters were concerned, was the hardest task of all. But Hephzibah could see the necessity of it. Without the radiation that the nuclear decimation would bring, one of the Daughters would never become god. But the evolutionary leap came at great sacrifice.

Hephzibah thought of the Mother, and Diana Nemorensis appeared. And as the Seraphim had dreamed, God asked her to hold back her hand and to let destiny unfold come what may. The female inhabitants of Tellus Mater had been made Hephzibah's to watch over. And she had been serious about her responsibilities to nurture and to protect them as they evolved. So, the Mother's request was unbearable.

"I beseech you, Mother," cried Hephzibah, "not to test me where the Daughters are concerned. I do not merely care for them. I love them. They are utterly vulnerable, and do not stand a chance in Hell of surviving without my help."

"Do you, my Daughter," asked Flora, as she appeared beside Hephzibah's throne overlooking the orb that was the manifestation of Tellus Mater resting on its golden stand, "trust in me so little?"

Hephzibah blushed, fell to her knees, and kissed the golden sandaled feet of God.

"Forgive me, Divine One," cried Hephzibah. "I beg forgiveness."

Flora passed the fingers of her right hand tenderly through Hephzibah's hair, as she used to when Hephzibah was a girl, and said, "Get up, Sheba."

Hephzibah stood with head bowed; embarrassed that she had questioned God the Creator of all things for even an instant.

Flora cupped her right hand beneath Hephzibah's chin and said, "Look at me, dearest daughter, for you have not offended me. You have done all things as you must as protector of this world and mother of millions, for the Tellusians surely have become your children. It is I who ask you to do the unusual, to forsake your duties and your instincts, and to let destiny unfold. And, for that, for holding back your hand when I know you desire to protect your charges, I beg forgiveness of you. It is the greatest sacrifice anyone can ask of a mother. I know because I was once asked to make the same sacrifice. Now you know how it feels."

Tears burst from Hephzibah at the Mother's apology before the fact. Hephzibah could not see as far ahead as Flora. She was a young goddess newly elevated from Seraph and had an eternity of learning ahead of her. For the Mother to apologize to her was magnanimous.

"My daughters have come so far," lamented Hephzibah, "only to end like this. It is all so sad."

"Yes," said Diana, "and no. Like a crocus pushing through late winter snow, new hope shall spring from this wanton destruction. The Daughters of Tellus Mater who survive this disaster, for they shall not all be killed, shall pick themselves up, dust themselves off, and start again. They are destined to join soon with the long forgotten other half of their species and give rise to a race of Angels of a kind who shall populate a new Haven. But one of these Daughters, separate from the others and virginal, is destined for something grander. See what I see."

Hephzibah saw God's vision.

"See the child ... there," said the Mother of Creation. "Her name is Ariel. And she is destined to evolve into god of a kind who shall create a new Haven on this world destroyed by Lucifer, reborn, and destroyed again by the Rancorians. This precious child is destined to hold dominion over an entire universe from a throne on this planet. And this Tellus Mater, this insignificant yet precious and wondrous pale blue dot spinning, orbiting, and transiting in the outskirts of the Milky Way is destined to become the center of the seventh universe. The Father has charged your sister Elektra to protect this child from all things while she undergoes her fragile metamorphosis. Moreover, far in the future, after the multiverse has burned itself to ash and Heaven too has grown old, it shall be her destiny to set us free."

Hephzibah looked through space and time at the farm girl. And the Goddess sensed what the girl sensed. She smelled air scented with the ozone of an approaching thunderstorm on a dry summer day, rich loam beneath a dried crust of topsoil, and the straw hat on her head. She tasted the sweat on her upper lip. She felt the pleasurable ache of taut muscles and the coolness of the breeze on her neck. She saw ears of lush corn hanging from tall stalks as far as the eye could see. And she heard what the girl heard. She heard the crunch and crush of cracked topsoil beneath her shoes, church bells ringing in the distance, and the girl's sweet voice as she sang the end of an English nursery rhyme from the olden time in step with the bells.

> Here comes a candle
> to light you to bed,
> And here comes a chopper
> to chop off your head.

The farm girl sliced a lush corn husk from its stalk with a curved handheld blade with varnished wooden handle, and tossed the harvested fruit into the wicker basket on the ground beside her. Then she suddenly looked up at the sky, at Heaven, and at Hephzibah, or so it seemed. And she smiled. It was as if she knew that she was being watched.

Hephzibah was taken aback, and then became angry and confused. "If this child is destined to destroy us, as you suggest," Hephzibah said defensively, "why do we not kill her first? Why should we allow her to become god?"

Diana smiled at her daughter. "Everything has a purpose, and a time," she said. "Even God in his Heaven and the Angels that make up the Chorus shall grow old and feeble one day and be in need of a merciful end to their existence. It is this child's purpose to eliminate us, you and me, and all of Heaven, when the time is right and we are too infirm to annihilate ourselves."

"I find it disturbing," said Hephzibah, "to contemplate such a thing or her as my, as our, executioner."

"And I," smiled Diana, "find great comfort in it."

Hephzibah hung her head in frustration. "Your will be done," she sobbed.

"I will stand beside you at the end, Sheba," said the Mother of all things, "as I stand beside you now to watch the destiny of this world unfold, for surely it must."

Chapter 20 - catalyst

Three days before Ariel's sixteenth birthday, her mother, Daffodil, and Thorn packed up a load of beef cows and headed for auction in the city. The heifers were choice, and her mother expected to get a good price. After the auction, she planned to buy much needed supplies, and a birthday present, and be back on the farm in time to celebrate the birthday girl.

But fate intervened.

The Rancorians invaded the Sol system in starships that resembled black scorpions. The ships were clunky, large, built for battle as they knew it, and practical. They were quickly positioned in geosynchronous orbit over every major Tellusian city. And shortly thereafter, they released their venom on an unsuspecting world.

"Kill them," ordered the Rancorian Commander. And so the bombardment of Tellus Mater began from an armada of starships orbiting the equator of the water world at twenty thousand clicks.

"Target all of their major cities," ordered the Rancorian Commander, "standard yield."

"Commander, we are receiving a signal from the Tellusians," said the communications officer. "They bid us greetings."

"Cities targeted and locked," said the weapons officer.

"Fire," said the Rancorian Commander dispassionately.

To the Commander, the Tellusians were dangerous. Their ideas of God, love, and peace were dangerous. They were a scourge the Rancorians had traveled light years to eliminate.

The Rancorian armada released one hundred projectiles before all was said and done. And until the very end, the Tellusians attempted to

communicate. But their initial greetings soon turned to pleas for the
Rancorians to stop their unprovoked attack.

It was Sunday morning. But instead of being in church, as they
usually were on Sunday morning, Ariel and Athena were in the corn
field harvesting by hand. A combination of problems conspired to put
them there that morning instead of in church in what others would later
construe as destiny. Nevertheless, they had been in the fields since four
and were in the midst of their work when the call to service rang out
from the churches in the distance that seemed to surround them. And
as was their custom when they heard the distinct bells, they sang an
English nursery rhyme from the old Earth of long ago passed along
through the verbal tradition. And it helped them pass the time and
forget their sore muscles.

"Oranges and lemons, say the bells of St. Clement's," sang Ariel.

And Athena responded with, "You owe us five farthings, say the
bells of St. Martin's."

When will you pay me?
Say the bells of Old Bailey.

When I grow rich,
Say the bells of Shoreditch.

When will that be?
Say the bells of Stepney.

But Athena's refrain was delayed for a moment while she listened.
In addition to the sound of bells on the wind was the shrill wail of a
siren.

Ariel sighed that their song should be so rudely interrupted. "Are
we expecting a storm?" she asked her friend and teacher.

"I do not know, says the great bell of Bow," sang Athena.

But before Ariel could give criticism on her friend's witticism with
a snide remark and an upturned nose, the horizon lit up in all directions
with a dozen colossal flashes. There was no escaping the blinding
light. There was no direction in which to turn. It was everywhere. So,
they looked down. They instinctively squinted, looked down, and
buried their eyes in the crook of an arm. And they screamed at the top

128

of their lungs at the painful intensity. It was so bright that it rendered their forearms transparent, to a degree, and allowed them to see radius and ulna through closed eyelids and two inches of flesh.

When the bright light subsided, once it slid through the visible spectrum from violet to red, they uncovered themselves and looked, in horror, at what the day wrought. The girls saw fireballs of sustained thermonuclear reaction rising, like monsters, over the corpses of what had been cities. And on the heels of the silent spectacle came the thunder of the blasts and the howling winds of explosion followed by the whine of implosion, as cities blown to smithereens were sucked back and tossed up into thick, black, mushroom clouds.

From out of those manmade pyronimbus abominations came fierce lightning, moaning thunder, and toxic snow. The crickets stopped chirping. The robins stopped singing. In the distance, church bells thrown from their steeples and melted to globs stopped ringing. And like a shroud, an eerie, surreal silence descended over the girls, the farm, and Tellus Mater.

The Rancorian Commander watched his monitor as one hundred cities were destroyed. From his God's eye view of the planet, the explosions reminded him of popcorn. And the residue reminded him of bubbling tar.

Ninety minutes after it began, it was over. But it had all been too easy. The Tellusians had put up no resistance.

"What kind of creature has no planetary defenses or weapons?" the Commander asked rhetorically. "How could our estimate of their strategic capabilities been so far off? Wait until I get my hands on the bureaucrat pencil pusher who thought up this one. We could have threatened them with harsh language and they would have ceased sending their damned signals into space. There was no need for this. It was a waste of resources. Nukes don't grow on trees. Remember that, Lieutenant. You never know where else you're going to need them."

The Rancorian Commander thought about his comment for a moment, but before a glimmer of remorse raised its ugly head, he shrugged his shoulders.

"Oh well," he said. "It's too late now. Set course for Rancor Prime, maximum velocity."

"Yes, Commander," said the flight navigator.

And so, as suddenly as the Rancorians arrived in the Sol system, they departed, leaving Tellus Mater ablaze, the Tellusian civilization destroyed, and the few who survived the direct attack dying from radiation.

As Ariel and Athena stared at the toxic mushrooms, they realized that Daffodil, Helen, and Thorn were gone.

"Do you think they got away?" asked Ariel.

"There wasn't time," said Athena.

"Do you think they're dead?" asked Ariel.

"Yes."

"Do you think they suffered?"

"No," said Athena. "It was fast, no pain, no worry, a flash of light."

Ariel nodded. She understood intellectually. But emotionally, her heart was ripped in two, for how could it not be? And her young life was changed forever.

She and Athena said a small prayer for God to take the souls of Akakallis, Akantha, and Helen, and the souls of everyone else who was killed that day. It seemed only right.

The initial and only battle of the *de facto* state of war that existed between the Rancorians and the Tellusians was executed and done shortly after it began. By the time the remaining few Tellusians recovered from the initial shock of the surprise attack and looked for the unknown enemy, the Rancorians had already departed Tellusian space.

The feeble few who possessed radio transmitters that had not been burned out by the electromagnetic pulses of the fission-fusion detonations sent out cries for help. They cried out into the darkness like blue jays in the uppermost branches of a tall poplar upon witnessing one of their own taken by a red-tailed hawk and eaten on the ground before them like a tasty treat. They cried out into the night because they did not know what else to do. They cried out because of the injustice that had just occurred even though their transmissions might take tens of thousands of years to reach the ears of a sympathetic soul.

Ariel and Athena returned to the farm house, heard the radio transmissions, and sighed.

"Why have you done this?" cried the Daughters of Tellus Mater over their radios. "Why?"

"Why has this happened?" Ariel asked Athena, trying to make some sense of nonsense. "It is all so sad."

"All I know," said Athena, "is that when God closes a door, she opens a window."

What had befallen Tellus Mater on that day was a sin in the eyes of God. Yet, she sensed that it was necessary if Ariel was to change. The secondary radiation from those blasts was vital to the young human. It would act as the catalyst to initiate her deific metamorphosis.

Shortly after witnessing the nuclear flashes and seeing the mushroom clouds, and realizing that her mother was gone, Ariel bled for the first time. After much trepidation, she finally became a woman. But it was a bitter pill. And her emotional anguish manifested in something more profound than merely the late onset of puberty. Ariel also bled from her hands, head, and feet.

"It is a sign," said Athena, recognizing the extraneous bleeding as deific stigmata.

Shortly after, Ariel fell into a deep sleep from which she could not awaken. And her somnambulism alarmed Athena. It was not what she expected when Xuxa assigned her to the task of overseeing Ariel's transformation. And in her gut she worried that something had gone horribly wrong. The Gabrielican Mother Superior tried to rouse the girl, but she would not respond. For all intents and purposes, it appeared that Ariel was the unfortunate victim of a massive stroke, and had fallen into a deep coma. And Athena was beside herself with worry, so much so that her faith was tested.

"It's all in God's hands now," she said.

The Mother Superior had to admit that things looked bleak. But Athena did not give up on the project. She fasted and prayed for guidance and strength. And she made Ariel as comfortable as possible while she waited for the inevitable.

Athena remained with Ariel day and night. She covered Ariel in a warm, hand-woven, gray wool blanket. She cleaned up the mess when Ariel defecated and urinated over her bed clothes and bedding repeatedly during the first twenty-four hours. After that, she merely stayed by her side, standing guard over a friend who could no longer protect herself from the elements.

Ariel remained in a coma for three days. Athena fully expected her skin to become dry and wrinkled during that time, since she was not hooked up to intravenous saline. She expected her cheeks to become sunken. But Ariel was vibrant. It reminded Athena of witness accounts of Bernadette Soubirous after death. In fact, Ariel appeared so alive that Athena was taken aback and checked the girl's eyes. But her pupils continued to be dilated, fixed, and unresponsive.

"It won't be long now," Athena said aloud, just to hear herself.

But Ariel did not pass. She transformed. In the middle of the night on the third day, while Athena slept in a chair at Ariel's bedside, the comatose young woman became covered in caterpillars. They swarmed to her sickbed from the farthest corners of the large farm. They spun their silk over her, silk they would otherwise have devoted to themselves. And when Athena awoke in the morning, she found Ariel encased in a cocoon. On the floor surrounding her bed were thousands of caterpillar corpses sacrificed in the name of Ariel. And so, the becoming began.

While Ariel drifted in her so-called vegetative state, she dreamed, although the textbooks said she should have no brain waves at all. She dreamed about the end. She dreamed about watching the end as it began from the porch of her farm house. Standing beside her, at her right elbow, was Elektra, Seraph, and Third Daughter of Paradise. Athena stood at her left elbow. Only she was not in the habit of a Gabrielican nun. She was an Angel with wings and a glowing nimbus behind her head, like the depictions of Angels in the *Book of Gabriel*.

In her dream, Ariel watched lightning strike everywhere, destroying buildings, and killing people. She knew in her heart of hearts that God was angry. Yet she was not afraid. She knew that she would not be punished. She would not be harmed. She had led a good life. She was true to God. And Elektra and Athena were there to protect her.

"This vision that we share," said Elektra, "is not what it seems."

Ariel smiled at her seraphic friend. "I know," she said.

"It is a symbol of things to come," said the Seraph, "and of what shall become of you."

"What is to become of me?" asked Ariel, as she jabbed her friend with her elbow.

"Something wonderful," said Elektra.

As Athena watched over the hardened cocoon of her young friend, the chrysalis began to glow. It glowed dimly, at first, like the red element atop an electric stove visible only in the dark. But it quickly became orange, and then yellow.

Athena stepped away from Ariel's sick bed and the heat that emanated from the chrysalis. She shielded her eyes from the glare of the cocoon that had become white hot like a newly formed ingot of rarified steel fresh from a blast furnace. For a moment, she panicked, thinking that the room would surely catch fire. She would be trapped, and perish. Then, amid the blinding glow of the chrysalis, Athena saw Elektra, and was overjoyed.

The Seraph was standing beside the sick bed with her right hand upon the white hot cocoon. Elektra sensed Athena's awe and fear and turned her face toward her, as the Gabrielican Mother Superior stood respectfully in the far corner.

"Do not fear," said the glowing, six-winged creature standing beside the chrysalis, "for I am here to watch over your friend during this time of becoming, just as you are. My name is Elektra. I am the Third Daughter of Paradise, and Seraph created by the Mother to sing the praises of the Father. I have been sent here by God Almighty to watch over the becoming of this precious child."

"Praise the Lord," said Athena.

"Indeed," said Elektra tenderly. "Come closer, Athena, for you and I are witness to a great change. Your friend, your Ariel, is in the midst of becoming the first of a new kind of creature. Like a caterpillar metamorphosing into a butterfly, she is becoming the next step in human evolution. She is becoming god."

The glow emanating from the chrysalis filled the room, the farmhouse, the farm, Tellus Mater, the Milky Way, and the seventh universe itself.

Then the chrysalis cracked open. And Ariel arose from the torn chamber like Xuxa rising from the bloody foam of the Great Lestan Sea. The nascent god stepped from the bed and stood beautiful beyond measure, naked, and radiant before the witnesses. And Athena sobbed at the sight of her.

Ariel had become god, not the God of the Old Testament, not Jesus Christ of the New. She was something different, yet similar. She had become a god in her own right, a god of our own. She had fulfilled an evolutionary destiny planted within the cold life that God Almighty sowed across the multiverse shaped like a starfish billions of years ago.

Ariel was the reason that human beings traveled into space to start with. She was the culmination of a four million year quest. Beyond the instinct to survive the global cataclysm foisted upon humanity by

133

Lucifer and his iron pyrite namesake was a desire to meet God, to be transformed by God, to become a god. But it was not done the way Hephaestia tried, by usurping God's authority, by rebelling against Heaven. It was obtained step by step in the natural order of things the way God intended.

Ironically, the catalyst for Ariel's change was the decimation heaved on the planet from a species ensconced in hatred who embraced death and destruction. It was from that dark ethos that Ariel sprang, like a purple crocus emerging through melting snow in springtime, to shine her light upon reality.

Elektra looked upon Ariel in awe and in admiration. She saw the being that Ariel had become as something greater than herself to a degree, as something similar, yet different. She saw her as baby, sister, and mother, and was amazed and honored to be there at her becoming.

The deific radiation emanating from Ariel filled the room with light and caused a change in Athena, as well. The chest of the Gabrielican nun glowed yellow through her habit. She transformed into an Angel with diaphanous wings, as Xuxa had foreseen. And thenceforth, Athena abandoned the Sisters of Atonement to become Ariel's handmaiden.

Elektra gazed at Ariel's large eyes with golden irises like her own and those of her sister Seraphim, and saw what she saw. Deep within those eyes, past the large pupils, past lenses and humors was the image of a solar system, our system, the Sol system. And traveling through it quickly away from Tellus was a flotilla of star ships.

Ariel saw Martian space ships pursuing the Rancorian armada, as they traveled past their world. She foresaw the men from the fourth planet blowing the Rancorian armada to smithereens. And she was glad.

In her thoughts, Ariel traveled to Rancor. She saw the murders, vivisections, and crucifixions of the Gabrielican nuns there, and her heart was saddened. She also witnessed the singular escape of Cassandra and Deesha, and it was a fresh breath of air amid the tightness that gripped her chest. She blinked, and the oil planet caught fire. It would burn until there was no oxygen left to sustain the combustion. But that would be long after all Rancorians had been killed.

Ariel looked out into the Milky Way galaxy, and wherever she found Rancorians, she wiped them out of existence. She had no patience for their cruelty. In her mind, they were a waste of space.

Ariel searched the Milky Way for every Tellusian missionary starship that had journeyed to a chosen world to spread the Word of the Mother through the *Book of Gabriel*. Where she found benevolence, her heart rejoiced. Where she found ambivalence, her heart sank with disappointment. But where she found malevolence, she became infuriated.

There simply was not enough good in the galaxy. She could see that now. She placed a blessing on worlds where the creatures there had kind dispositions and welcomed the Gabrielican missionaries honestly and openly. She placed a curse on worlds throughout the galaxy where the indigenous creatures devoured the Gabrielicans. She made them so confused that they devoured themselves, and that included the harvesters that Alterna launched toward Tellus Mater. They were destined to run out of fuel, have a communications breakdown, and drift in the interstellar void until they cannibalized themselves. And she destroyed those worlds where she found vicious intelligence. On those cruel worlds, the inhabitants had chosen to be evil. And she heaved the wrath upon them that only a vengeful god could bring. She struck them down with bolts of lightning thrown from angry, black clouds. She filled their merciless hearts with terror as the evil creatures ran for cover. She watched them as they scattered like ants. But, in the end, they could not escape her.

She finally understood her dream where she stood on the porch beside Elektra. The dream was not about God Almighty throwing lightning bolts at the panicked populace. It was about her becoming god. It was about her administering absolute justice across the Milky Way, and across all of the galaxies in the seventh universe.

In that instant, all was vindicated in the great mind of God Almighty. He viewed Ariel and her vengeance and knew, in his heart of hearts, that her actions were true. She did what he could not. She was what he was not. From Adam and Eve to the present, all had occurred for a reason. It was to get to that point in the here and now where Abraxas could finally unburden his heart. And so, God swept his right hand before his eyes and wiped the slate clean. All past infractions were forgiven. Humanity was finally forgiven. And the male survivors of a corrupt Earth of long ago who journeyed to Mars in order to survive the decimation that asteroid Lucifer wrought were forgiven too.

In the four million years that had passed, the men from Mars had changed. They had mutated. They had evolved. Like the Tellusians, the Martians had become Homo angelicus. As kindred spirits, they had wrecked vengeance upon the victorious Rancorian fleet. They regretted not arriving in time to protect Tellus Mater from the Rancorian attack. But, then again, they were never destined to arrive in time. For, if they had, Ariel would never have become god.

After a four million year absence, it was the destiny of the evolved men from Mars to return to an Earth resurrected and to the bosoms of the surviving Daughters of Tellus Mater. It was time that the genders of the human race were reunited. And so, the Martians would begin their return to the home world spoken of in legend and seen every night hanging like a pale, blue dot amid the stars.

Chapter 21 - retribution

The brilliant hydrogen bomb flashes instantly penetrated Earth's atmosphere and traveled into space, as hemispheric rings of light expanding outward at one hundred and eighty-six thousand miles a second. The ever increasing photon rings took a little over one and a quarter seconds to hit the moon. They took four minutes to touch Mars, thirty-five minutes to caress Jupiter and a little over five hours to whisper past Saturn, Uranus, Neptune and Pluto. And from there, they took the better part of a year to reach the rocky environs of the Oort cloud, at the farthest reaches of the Sol system and one third of the way to the next star.

The Martians witnessed the flashes four minutes after the crimes were committed against the Daughters of Tellus Mater, and set upon the Rancorians like hounds to hares shortly after their black scorpions departed. The Men from Mars had been monitoring communications between the Tellusians and the Rancorians for years. And they did not trust the aliens of Rancor. The Rancorians had learned the Tellusian language, which was a dialect of twenty-first century Earth English. But they spoke it awkwardly and disingenuously, unintentionally revealing their true agenda. Martian linguists and Psychologists were convinced that the Rancorians secretly hated the Tellusians and might attack them. So, they prepared themselves. The men from Mars swore that they would protect their Tellusian sisters. But they failed. They did not act quickly enough.

The Martian space ships were designed to look like wisps of wind. They looked fragile, but were not. When the men from Earth abandoned their home so long ago just before asteroid Lucifer decimated the third planet from the sun, their twenty-first century space ships were sophisticated for the time. But now, four million years later, those space ships that brought the men from Earth to Mars were considered museum pieces. They were quaint anachronisms, primitive cans with antiquated propulsion systems. And young Martian engineers marveled at how the ships ever made the ten month journey from Earth to Mars at all. They viewed old drawings of the Nina, Pinta, and Santa Maria, the ships that Columbus used to cross the Atlantic ocean from the old world to the new, in the same light. Now, the journey across the Atlantic, if there was such a thing, could be accomplished in the blink of an eye. And the voyage from Tellus Mater to Mars took mere seconds.

Yet, the Rancorians arrived at Tellus Mater before the Martians could stop them, which had more to do with Martian politics than technological prowess or proximity.

For four million years, the Martians had lived on their world, or rather beneath their world, hidden from the scans of passing alien ships beneath thick lead shields. Unlike the Tellusians, they broadcast no messages into space. They did not announce their presence. For all intents and purposes, they wished their planet to appear hostile, windswept, and uninhabited.

Martian youngsters, when they were taught astronomy, would inevitably ask the question: "Why don't we communicate with other worlds? Why don't we communicate with Tellus Mater? Why are we silent?" And their teacher would point to a drawing on the wall depicting Cortez and the indigenous natives of the Americas. "Look what happened to the Indians," he would say. And that would be that.

When the approaching Rancorian fleet scanned the Sol system from outside the Kuiper belt, the only organized and patterned electromagnetic waves they detected came from Tellus Mater. Their threat assessment of the system indicated minimal to no resistance to their planned attack. So, they proceeded. But, like a trap door spider, the Martians sensed the Rancorians as they passed, and followed close behind, mere seconds behind, with the intent of destroying the Rancorians between Mars and Tellus. But God is in the details. And those few seconds of miscalculation dealt a devastating blow to Mother Earth.

The Martian Commander, a young man of exceptional intelligence and passion called Alexander, a twenty-one year old beauty with the Macedonian blood of Alexander the Great running through his veins, had become complacent. He had assumed that his people, the Sons of

Mars, were so superior to the Rancorians that he would have all the time in the world to pursue the enemy and to destroy them half way between Mars and Tellus Mater. And so, he had slept in on the expected day of Rancorian transit. Future historians would comment that something as self-indulgent as sleeping in would result in the catastrophic loss of several million Tellusian lives. They would blame the Martian's over reliance on superior technology in lieu of sound strategy as the contributing factor.

Some historians would even go so far as to say that young Alexander and his family were lazy dilettantes playing at being demigods with their power rings and fancy space ships that looked like Pharaoh's barges on the Nile or garish, Mardi Gras parade floats rather than nuts and bolts technology designed for a serious purpose. But the reach of Alexander's family was great. And those historians who dared speak out against the favored son, even in the future, would be dealt with harshly and swiftly. The writings of these historians would never be published. The originals would be destroyed, or severely redacted to make them incomprehensible, or purposefully misfiled, lost in the annals of antiquity until nature itself oxidized the media upon which the critical words were written or stored.

When God looked at Alexander, as the men from Mars rushed to the aid of the women from Tellus Mater, the Master Architect of the Multiverse saw an exceptional young man blessed with an array of virtues and cursed with a litany of short comings. He was better than Adam. He was new and improved. He was evolved. Yet, he was still plagued by flaws that kept him human.

God looked within Alexander's genes and saw that he and his people had become Homo angelicus like the women on their neighboring world. It had taken the Martians four million years to reach that point; whereas, it had only taken the Tellusians approximately ten thousand, when travel at relativistic velocities and the help of the Mother of Creation were factored into the equation. And it pleased God greatly to see that mankind had survived and flourished even in desolation and isolation.

So much corporeal life throughout the Milky Way galaxy had faltered long before that point. So much intelligent life in the universe had shown potential yet fallen by the wayside. The multiverse itself was a testament to God's hope and dismal disappointment in the evolution of cold, corporeal existence to rarefied ethereal manifestation. So, when Abraxas looked at Alexander, God the Father was less critical than future historians. He saw the big picture for only he could. He knew that destiny was about to prove him wrong.

God had lost faith in mankind long ago as ungodly creatures, when Adam and Eve disobeyed his simple rules in the Garden. He had lost faith a second time when the people of Moses broke every one of the commandments carved in stone atop Mount Horeb. He lost faith again after he gave mankind a third chance and sent his Son to teach them to love one another. That time they killed God. They hoisted him upon a cross of olive wood and crucified him like a common criminal. Now, here, with these supposedly evolved men from Mars rushing to save the other half of their species from certain extinction, Abraxas saw altruism. And it engendered such new hope in him that he gave human beings another chance.

The Martian fleet engaged the Rancorian armada after the damage was done to Tellus Mater and the treacherous aliens were on their way out of the Sol system. The Rancorians saw the Martians coming after them and attacked first. They locked nuclear missiles on the Martians and fired. As a second line of defense, they dropped nuclear proximity mines behind them. Then the Rancorian Commander gave the order to take up defensive positions amid the detritus of Saturn's outermost ring.

The Martians systematically neutralized and swept aside the approaching nuclear missiles and the silent, waiting, nuclear mines. They tracked the ion trails of the black scorpions like hounds upon a fox and found the enemy spaceships hiding behind the spinning, translating, and vibrating boulders of Saturn's E ring, powered down and running silently to avoid detection like submarines out of Earth's twentieth century past, but to no avail.

"Commence attack. Fire. Fire. Fire." said Alexander quietly, as he sat upon his ornately carved throne of Rosewood and red velvet aboard the Martian Command ship. And from there he viewed the ensuing spectacle of Will-o'-the-wisps, with their blazingly fast yet cool, radiation impervious, nanodiamond electronics, attacking black scorpions, with their slow, clunky and overheated vacuum tube technology, to the divine music of Pachelbel's Canon in D Major.

Thoughts, magnified through Moorcockian power rings on the fingers of the Martian commanders, activated weapons that appeared as ephemeral as dandelion fluffs, but were as stalwart as brick walls.

Plasma hotter than the sun scorched from the Martian ships and cut the black scorpions to pieces. And so, the dreaded Rancorians lost half of their armada in the first thirty seconds of *the retribution*, or so the turkey shoot in the E-ring came to be called.

To the Rancorians, the Martian ships did not appear to be space vessels at all. The Rancorian computers classified them as *unknown*. Their propulsion system was unknown. Their method of shielding was unknown. Their weapons were unknown. When the Rancorians attempted to scan the Martian ships, their scanners became confused because nothing about the Martian ships registered as solid. The ships didn't even register as in phase with reality. So, confronted with an enemy unknown with superior technology, the few Rancorian ships that survived the initial half minute attack got out of Dodge.

But the Martians did not leave it at that. They did not want the Rancorians to revisit their Tellusian sisters. So, they followed the sinister and ungodly creatures as they retreated to the outskirts of the Sol system in preparation for a jump into hyperspace. They caught up with them just beyond Neptune. And they blew them to smithereens destined to forever orbit Sol from the dark, outer reaches of the Kuiper Belt and the Oort cloud.

Chapter 22 - revelation

The Third Princess of Paradise journeyed with Ariel and her angelic handmaiden across the extradimensional expanse that exists beyond solar systems, galaxies, and universes, and steered them toward Heaven itself.

They sailed aboard a small, wooden ship of ancient Macedonian design created with a thought within Ariel's extralucent mind to serve a purpose that was unnecessary but was esthetically pleasing. The Pegasus, or so she dubbed it because it was a noble name for an intrepid ship, was painted ecru and ivory. The sturdy craft had the wooden head of a sea horse aft and its tail astern, with ornate eyes on its bow, and three keels beneath resembling the fins of a fish.

Elektra manned the tiller and steered the vessel through the ether above a stormy, cobalt blue Celestial Sea against a backdrop of black clouds. Athena manned rigging and sail. And Ariel stood aft fearlessly and half naked, her Doric chiton blown off her torso by the wind, its linen collected at her forearms and grasped by her hands, and her fiery-orange hair blown forward in the direction of her destiny. And, for a time, her body was stained cobalt blue in sympathy with the Sea.

As Ariel, Athena, and Elektra neared Heaven, sitting like an island oasis amid the vast cobalt blue Celestial Sea, they were joined in the chaos through which they flew by Choirs of Angels. The heavenly creatures sensed the arrival of the new god, the new Angel, and the Princess of Heaven, and rowed out into the aquamarine shallows to escort them to safe harbor.

Like the natives of a tropical island, the Angels surrounded Pegasus with dugout canoes of their own design manufactured from the fabric of energy itself. And they threw their best wishes, blessings, and prayers into the shallow, aquamarine waters around the ship. They

dove into the shallow chaos and smiled at Ariel as Pegasus flew past.
They waved at her like the perpetual children they were standing in the
crowd on the edge of a passing parade, and sang her name. Angels
handed her parrot feathers of cerulean and lime that she placed in her
hair. Others handed her Calla lilies that she collected in a bouquet.
And in sympathy with her new surroundings, Ariel's body also turned
aquamarine like the shallow Celestial Sea surrounding Heaven within
which the Angels swam. She smiled at the Angels and waved back.
And she would have stopped to talk with the natives, but Elektra looked
steadfast into the future, and held their course straight and true. And
so, they navigated to Heaven, to the Citadel, and directly to God's door.

Pegasus docked high in the clouds atop Mount Ecclesia, far above
the amber fields of grain below so recently soaked with the blood of
Angels from the Great War of Heaven. Ariel pulled her linen dress up
over her shoulders once again. Then the external door to God's throne
room opened, as if they were expected for indeed they were. And
Ariel, Athena, and Elektra stepped from the little ship onto the
flagstones of a high patio overlooking the perfection of a farm in
Tuscany, and walked toward and through the nine foot, ornately carved,
rosewood doors of the deific throne room to meet God Almighty
himself.

Abraxas looked Ariel up and down. She stood before him attired in
a simple chiton and sandals, with skin stained aquamarine and cobalt
blue like the Celestial Sea, with cerulean and lime parrot feathers in her
hair, and with a bouquet of Calla lilies crooked in her right arm. And
he couldn't be more pleased. She was as he had always imagined. For
how else would she be? She was the culmination and the manifestation
of everything he had ever hoped for when he tossed the rudimentary
particles of cold life out into the inhospitable chaos of the multiverse
shaped like a starfish. Now here was the evolved cold life back to greet
him, to pay homage to him, and to thank him at last.

"Welcome, my child," he said to Ariel, as he reached out his right
hand for her to take.

But she nervously handed him the bouquet of Calla lilies instead, as
an offering. And he was momentarily startled. But when he thought
about it, he was greatly pleased by her gesture, and proud of this new
god. And so, he ordered the lilies placed in a tall, glass vase of tepid
water beside his throne where all could see the symbolic gift of the
creation to the creator.

144

Then God said, "Give me your hand, child." And Ariel placed her right hand delicately into his, like a dancer at a masque. And God Almighty twirled her around him on the floor of the throne room.

"And who is this Angel I see before me?" he asked, looking over Ariel's right shoulder at Athena.

"Athena is my handmaiden," said Ariel, "recently elevated to Angel by a similar mechanism that elevated me to god."

"Yes," said Abraxas, "I can see that. Welcome, Athena. You have been much talked about, and most highly acclaimed by an Angel that I believe you are acquainted with. You have been expected."

Abraxas looked directly at Athena, and she lowered her gaze.

"Look upon me, child," he said, "for you are allowed to do so with my permission."

"Yes, Lord," she wept.

"A nascent Angel named Xuxa told us a wondrous tale which pleased me greatly. She waits for you in the Crystal Palace. Go to her now. There is much she is dying to tell you."

Athena bowed before God Almighty and departed.

God then faced Elektra.

"Look upon me, Third Daughter of Heaven," said Abraxas.

Elektra looked at God.

"Dearest Elektra," he said, "when I need something done right, I send in the Seraphim. And so, I turned to you to see this child of Earth through this delicate transition. And here, you have delivered the successful fruits directly to my door. Thank you. You have done a fine job. But now, I relieve you. You are free to rejoin the Chorus. We shall talk later."

"Thank you, Father,' said Elektra. "I stand relieved." She bowed before God, but before she departed, she turned to Ariel and said, "I wish you well."

"As I do you," said Ariel.

Elektra bowed to Ariel too, and left, shutting the doors of the throne room behind her.

Ariel spun at the fingertips of God Almighty. And the throne room spun around her. She focused on God as she spun. And as she did so, he was, at once, God of the Old Testament, Jesus Christ himself, and Flora the Mother of Creation. He was the Trinity. He was the One. He was one God seen in three manifestations, in perhaps millions of manifestations over the course of space and time throughout the multiverse. And she sobbed at the revelation. She had always suspected as much. Education and faith had informed her, but she had not believed wholeheartedly. Now she saw for herself that it was true.

"Yes," said God.

"Yes," said Ariel.

"And now you," said God. "It is truly marvelous."

"One with you?" she asked.

"Of us, but not one with us," he laughed with joy. "You are a new becoming and beginning, a new being, and a new form. Is it not *Mirabile visu?*"

God stopped his spinning, took a deep, long breath, and spoke with her seriously.

"My child," he said, "you are the first of your kind and perhaps the only. You are my miracle baby, and cherished beyond measure. You are my creation, my joy, and my suffering, and proof to Heaven that seeding cold life into the multiverse, so long ago, was worthwhile. But there is no throne for you here in Heaven. You must create a New Haven, and a new reality to go with it."

"I am uncertain," said Ariel, "that I can achieve such a thing."

"Don't be," said the manifestation of Flora standing before her. "For within you exists the fecundity necessary to create anything and everything only better than I did, than we did. And, by your will, you shall."

The manifestation of Adonai and a very pregnant Hephzibah stood hand in hand and deeply in love before Ariel.

"Love life," said Adonai.

"Create life," said Hephzibah, "and program basic goodness into that life. That would please us greatly."

Adi and Sheba smiled at Ariel, and she smiled back.

Then Ariel fell to her knees because it was all so much, so fast.

"Father, Mother, Sister, Brother," she prayed to the glowing orb that hovered before her, "I ask for your blessing before I start this great undertaking."

And she received it without hesitation. Their energy surged into her, and completed her.

Ariel blinked.

And when she opened her eyes, she was no longer in God's throne room. She instead found herself kneeling on succulent, green grass between two rows of vines amid the vineyard of Heaven. And standing before her was the Queen of Heaven herself, as Flora, forever beautiful and young, dressed in gold crown, an ornate red velvet gown with gold brocade, and golden sandals.

Flora gave Ariel her right hand and the neophyte god rose to her feet. The Mother of Creation removed the sympathetic aquamarine and cobalt blue stains from the young god's flesh. Then Flora slid Ariel's chiton from her shoulders. And the linen gown slipped down the girl's perfect olive skin into a crumpled pile at her feet.

As Ariel watched, Flora slipped out of her golden sandals. She undid her red velvet gown, and let it slip to the ground too. She removed her gold crown and placed it upon her footwear. Then she took Ariel by the hand, and the naked Mother of Creation and the naked god of the seventh universe, with their fiery-orange hair ablaze, walked the grassy rows of the vineyard together. And the Queen of Heaven and her protégé generated life with every deific footfall and touch.

Sensing the deific presence of the gods, dormant roots pumped water and nutrients up xylem and into crown, trunk, cordons, arms, and fruiting spurs. Lime green shoots and tendrils stretched out to kiss them as they passed, and pollen exploded from anthers and stuck to stigmas.

Diana Nemorensis smiled at Ariel as they walked the vine rows because all was truly fine, in every sense, with the Little Kingdom and beyond. When she peered within Ariel's extralucent mind, she saw herself there as the smallest of seeds sown so long ago grown now into a majestic oak. In every sense, Ariel was truly her daughter. Moreover, Ariel was Flora reinvented, the child better than the parent. And it pleased the Mother to see it.

Diana knew what the nascent god was going through at that very instant, and would go through during her first billion years. It would be an exciting time for her. And she envied Ariel. At the same time, she pitied her. She knew that the girl would not make the same mistakes she had. But she would still make mistakes. And she would suffer over them, as would the creatures she created or stewarded who were impacted by her *faux pas*.

"Enough of this excursion," said Diana. And in the blink of an eye, she and Ariel were fully clothed and having afternoon tea, as they sat upon Kelly green high-backed chairs in a sitting room paneled in rosewood.

"What do you see," asked Flora, "when you look at your refreshment?"

Ariel stared at her cup of Darjeeling and observed a thin layer of ecru froth atop the hot, burnt umber liquid.

"I see," said the new deity, as she stared at the froth with golden irises and her mind traveled into it, into what seemed like a whirl of bubbles but was actually the microscopic realm of billions of galaxies, "a universe in a tea cup."

"A latent universe," said the Mother of Creation, "a *tabula rasa* awaiting the Hand of God. One day you will choose yours. You will create life within it, nurture it, and protect it, as I have done with the multiverse shaped like a starfish on the floor of the Mandala Room of Heaven."

Ariel laughed out loud, sucked the unformatted, Darjeeling universe into her great maw, and swallowed the rarefied liquid that was not really hot tea at all, but rather a thought in the mind of the Mother converting energy into matter for their fleeting amusement.

"Did you not see, Mother," she asked, "when you looked within me, what I had in mind?"

"I surely did not."

"It is my wish to preside over the universe of my origin. I desire nothing else. I believe it is my destiny. May I do so with your permission?"

"Who am I to stand in the way of destiny?" said the Mother of Creation. "You may do so, child, with my blessing. It is a good universe with much life to it still before it extinguishes, as all things must in time. Steward it well. Do great good, for you have it within you to do so. I am pleased."

"As am I, Mother."

"Let me do one more thing before you go because I sense you are eager to depart as all young people are. I desire to bestow upon you a new name befitting your status and bespeaking your lineage. I so dub thee Ariel Nemorensis, god of the seventh universe within creation, and Daughter of Diana for all time."

As the Mother of Creation spoke Ariel's new name, an ornate deific tattoo appeared on Ariel's back from shoulder to shoulder and from neck to ascending superior spine so all of the Angels in Heaven and elsewhere would recognize her as god of the seventh universe. And upon the palm of Ariel's right hand, the Mother emblazoned the newly imagined deific Seal of Ariel linked to her own so others would know that she was blessed by Heaven.

Ariel was taken aback by Flora's generosity and kindness. The young god rushed into the arms of the Mother of Creation and buried her face in a bosom that had provided the milk for trillions of galaxies.

"Thank you, Mother," Ariel sobbed. "Thank you. I am grateful."

Chapter 23 - axis mundi

Ariel was invited to live in Heaven with Diana, Abraxas, Adonai and Hephzibah, and to administer her kingdom from there. But she chose a different location. It was her desire to exist within the universe that was hers to steward. And so, she returned to the seventh universe and to the planet she loved, to Tellus Mater.

Ariel returned to a planet scarred and scorched by hydrogen bomb blasts and the firestorms that followed. She returned to a dead, dying, and irradiated world, and to a people betrayed, her people, traumatized from an unprovoked attack from a supposed friend. And, with the help of Agatha, Gia, and Sophia who Hephzibah released from her *sanctum sanctorum*, she transformed the incinerated sphere into her version of Heaven.

Ariel arrived as she left dressed in a Doric chiton aboard Pegasus, with Elektra at the tiller, and Athena in charge of the rigging and the sail. The Mother of Creation had given Elektra the choice of remaining in Heaven or going with Ariel to be an ambassador and a missionary from the old Heaven to the New Haven. Elektra chose the challenge that Ariel represented even though it meant isolation for a very long time from the Heaven she knew and loved and the Mother she adored. And Flora granted her request. So, the god of the Seventh Universe, the Third Daughter of Heaven, and the First Angel of Haven exited the extradimensional expanse that exists beyond systems, galaxies, and universes, and completed their journey from Heaven to Tellus Mater.

In their wake came Xuxa and a chorus of Uteran Angels. From now on, every Uteran struck down by lamia and reborn as an Angel from the bloody froth of the Great Lestan Sea would think herself to Tellus Mater to serve the new god. It was their destiny.

Ariel blinked and they arrived in the post-apocalyptic shadow of the Rancorian altercation soon after they departed. Everywhere around them, the devastated cities bubbled and burned. And acrid, black smoke surged upward and formed dark, ominous, pyrocumulus clouds that flashed and rumbled, and from which radioactive detritus and deadly rain fell.

Ariel blinked again and removed the seventh universe, her universe, the universe that was hers to do with as she pleased, from its station in the Mandala Room of Heaven. And in doing so she changed God's multiverse shaped like a starfish for all time.

She blinked again and dissolved the Perpetual Stream falling from Heaven and cutting across the seventh universe on its way to Hell. And, in doing so, she broke the connection that the seventh universe had with each deific realm. She pulled the plug on the negative influence that the ancient war with its demons and Devil had upon the countless worlds under her purview. And like a teenager leaving home to set out on her own, she cut herself and the seventh universe off from Heaven, as well. She needed time to establish her own Paradise, to clean house, to imagine, and to create.

The new god raised her right hand, whose palm was emblazoned with the Seal of Ariel linked with the Seal of Diana, swung if gracefully from left to right before her field of view, and erased the worldwide post-nuclear devastation. And she replaced it with a pristine Eden of her imagining. It was not the Father's Eden redone with Adam and Eve, the Tree of Life, the Tree of Knowledge of Good and Evil, and Satan to tempt the human woman. It was not God Almighty's Heaven with the evil and good twins Hephaestia and Hephzibah of the Seraphim. It was the world reborn without evil or temptation in it. It was Ariel's version of Heaven perfected. And she called it Haven.

And the Seal of God Almighty tattooed upon the palms of the Uteran Angels was burned off with a thought and replaced with the tattooed Seal of Ariel, so that the Angels could perform miracles in her name and in the name of Haven on Earth.

Long ago, before Galileo Galilei with his observations of the night sky revealed that the planets of the Sol system orbited the sun, the commonly held belief was that the Earth was the center of the universe. Now, with god in residence upon the small, water world, what was once called Earth, New Earth, and Tellus Mater became the *axis mundi*, the center of the seventh universe indeed. Once upon a time, all roads in the civilized world led to Rome. Now, all roads in the known universe led to Haven.

During the first deific week, Ariel witnessed the reunion of the men from Mars with the cesium-irradiated women from Tellus Mater. She had romantic notions about the two halves of the evolved human race becoming whole again for the first time in four million years. But those notions were quickly dashed. The Martian side of Homo angelicus, unbridled after so long, surged upon the crippled Tellusians like locusts. Like the monkey boys they were that existed just beneath their façade of civility and behind their power rings and sophisticated technology, the Martian males raped every Tellusian female they encountered. Their polymorphous perversion spread around the planet like the plague. And like the wave of Amarantine that crashed at the feet of God Almighty at the death of Hephzibah during the War of Heaven so long ago, *Love Lies Bleeding* crashed at the foot of Ariel's deific throne to inform her that something was terribly wrong in her own house.

Ariel had romantically expected the Martians to court the Tellusians, to become engaged to them, to marry them, with her blessing, and to produce children within a family structure on her Haven. She had not expected the males to rape and to sodomize the women, to engage in multiple, unsanctioned coupling, or to beat them into submission. And she had not expected the sexual encounters to be promiscuous, recreational, and violent. But they were. And it offended her.

During the second deific week of Ariel's reign, she witnessed the raped Daughters of Tellus Mater give birth to a race of Demons. And she was so offended by their creation that she thought the abominations out of existence. She thought the offending Martians and the Tellusians who were tempted by their evil and succumbed to their perversion out of existence, as well. Then she extended her will out into the universe at the speed of thought and destroyed evil wherever she found it.

The surviving Martians, respectful of god and mindful of women as human beings and their equals, if not superiors, courted the women from Tellus Mater. They married them in the sight of god. And the couples made love as husband and wife.

During the third deific week, Ariel witnessed the Tellusians give birth to babies who glowed with divine light, with her light. The children of Mars and Tellus Mater grew at an astonishing rate. And at the end of seven days, they were fully formed Angels with glowing nimbuses and deific wings. And their parents were in awe and proud and saddened because they realized that their progeny were destined to serve Ariel and would be leaving them soon. And so they did.

The Angels left their parents and were sent out, by Athena, among the galaxies of the seventh universe, as emissaries. These new Messengers spread the story of Ariel's great becoming, and informed creatures everywhere that Ariel was god of the new age. They taught her commandments. And they spread her deific message of love.

Acceptance of Ariel, as god, was absolute. Those who refused to accept her as god were turned to salt. Those who thought they could believe in her when it was convenient and believe in whatever they wanted the rest of the time were turned into worms. But those who believed in her, and who accepted her simple commandments, lived long, prosperous lives.

As per Ariel's wishes, Agatha, Gia, and Sophia saw to it that every habitable planet in the seventh universe had an antenna placed upon it designed to transmit the prayers of its occupants to Ariel instantly, beyond the physical constraints of space and time. Each antenna was a *columna cerului*, a celestial and a geographical pole pointing toward god in her Haven.

At first blush, the pink antenna of god looked organic, possessing features of both animal and vegetable kingdoms. But, although Ariel's antenna looked so, it was neither, nor was it merely technology. It was a creation of god herself constructed from the pure energy of extralucent mind transformed by will into matter, of a kind, that existed simultaneously in eleven dimensions both in and out of reality.

Ariel's antenna rose like an Egyptian obelisk from the sacred pool that provided sustenance to the four rivers of creation that she established on every world. The antenna stretched up out of the pure water like a large pink onion with progressively smaller onions stacked atop it. Growing out of the onion at the base and reaching toward the sky were pink protuberances resembling the tentacles of a cuttlefish. Growing out of the second tier were branches resembling sheaths of wheat. They pointed upward still to stalks capped with spheres resembling the eyes of a lobster. And so the organic antenna extended upward past lily stamens toward a tapered tip that resembled the singular, tightly twisted horn of a fabled beast with a direct link to God.

Ariel's antenna appeared feminine and masculine, natural and manmade, religious and secular. Like Diana's grove in the forest, and her one time tree of Bloodwood, it was the new *sanctum sanctorum*. But it was accessible to all. It was the center of every microcosm of every world. It was the planet's navel, its *omphalos*. It was the alter stone upon which sacrifices were made and prayers were transmitted. And it was the receiver through which god spoke to her people everywhere.

And so, word of her spread throughout the seventh universe delivered by deific emissaries who told of the god Ariel who lived near the inner rim of the Orion arm of the Milky Way galaxy in the Sol system on the planet Haven.

During a quiet moment in her deific duties, Ariel and Athena returned to the farmstead. Ariel picked up a shovel and dug a hole in the center of the farmyard. And within it she planted an oak sapling in memory of her mother. Equidistant from it, Athena planted two chestnut trees, one for Daffodil and one for Thorn in her side. Ariel and her First Angel said a blessing over the trees and imagined the transmigrated souls of their dearly departed entering and living within the plants. And Ariel arranged for Gabrielican nuns to run the farm, in perpetuity, and to venerate the Three Sisters, or so the trees came to be called.

Ariel sat beneath a scarlet velvet canopy upon her matching padded *acathedra* within the confines of her deific sanctuary and listened to trillions of prayers simultaneously, in real time, as they came in through her antenna system. And she answered the prayers simultaneously, for only a god could. No longer would anyone or any creature in the seventh universe ever feel alone. No longer would they feel that their deity had abandoned them. In every sense of the word, she was the living god. And she continued to be so until every star and every galaxy in the seventh universe burned itself out.

Ariel was destined to return to Heaven far in the future, as the end of days approached, and to renew her contact with Father and Mother. But, by then, they would be hard pressed to remember her. She had hoped that the Father would dance with her once more. She had hoped that the Mother would disrobe with her, take her by the hand, and walk naked and natural with her amid the vine rows, as they once had. She had hoped that their deific hearts would be filled with joy at the sight of her. But it was not to be. There would be no cause for celebration across the face of Heaven at the return of the prodigal daughter and god. There would be only confusion, fear, and sadness. Her return would merely mark the beginning of the end for all concerned for only she among them would have the clarity of extralucent mind and the strength of will to do what had to be done.

Chapter 24 - vindication

The Martians and the Tellusians stood hand in hand in the early light of dawn, as Lily and Eve had once stood to commemorate their return to Earth after their fifty-six year voyage at ninety-nine per cent of the speed of light to Andromeda and back while the Earth cooled for four million years from its destruction at the hands of asteroid Lucifer. The evolved and reunited men and women of an Earth destroyed, reborn, renamed, and conflagrated once more stopped to listen to the robin's song at dawn.

The Martians knew that there was a robin inside every one of them. The Tellusians knew that there were robins within them too. Within the genome of the mutated human race was the stored, deactivated DNA of its reptilian predecessors and their avian descendants, of the first among their kind: archaeopteryx, and of the robins that were brought into the future aboard starship Noah so long ago. The Martians and the Tellusians were proud of their common bond with each other and with robins. After so many millennium of thinking that human beings were superior to every creature on the planet, pain and suffering finally transformed them. They learned to see. Without their moral blindness, they saw robins for what they truly were. When the Martians and the Tellusians looked at robins with their new eyes they saw them as their elders. And they saw themselves as their children. So, ever after, robins were given the respect that they deserved.

Unlike the single robin that sang in the apple orchard before Lily and Eve and the congregation of one hundred thousand Daughters of Tellus Mater on that cool spring day so long ago, now mother robins and their daughters and sisters serenaded the survivors with their early morning song. Like choirs of Angels, choirs of robins praised Ariel god of the seventh universe for the great honor of being alive, for the new day, and for the world re-created.

Ever since Xuxa's ascendance from Utera to Angel and Ariel's transformation from Daughter to god, the veneration of robins had grown because the surviving Tellusians believed that robins would ascend soon too. So, the Daughters stopped what they were doing when robins sang. They took off their straw hats. Out of great respect, they listened, prayed, and watched as choirs of the ancient birds sang their evening and morning songs in praise of god. They bowed their heads as choirs of robins congregated to sing dolorous prayers over the bodies of the deceased. And observers broke down and sobbed when choirs of robins surrounded the birthing women from the water world seeded by the men from the desert planet and sang the most joyous prayers ever heard at the miraculous birth of Angels.

And, at long last, everything was as it was meant to be.

Beside the old plaque hanging on the outcrop of red granite near where Noah once landed so long ago, there hung a new plaque. The old inscription read: "A rocky road leads to the stars." And the new inscription read: "A rocky road leads to God."

Everyone knew that the new inscription had a double meaning. It referred to belief. But it also referred to what they had become, to what the human race had evolved into since the first steps of hominids in Olduvai Gorge to now, here, with them, and with their children. Both sexes had evolved independently into Homo angelicus after Lucifer's decimation. The Rancorian adversity brought them together. And their coupling gave rise to a miraculous race of Angels. But the greatest miracle of all went one giant step further. The radiation from the Rancorian assault stimulated the spontaneous mutation of Ariel into god.

Elektra, Third Princess of Heaven, and sister to Hephzibah, Thea, and Arabella had been there and had watched over Ariel while she transformed. She had delivered her to Heaven so that the neophyte god could receive the blessings of Father, Mother, Sister, and Brother. And until the end of time, she was destined to tell the story of Ariel's miraculous becoming.

Hephzibah, one-time goddess of Tellus Mater, was beside herself with joy at the elevation of Ariel to god of a kind, and the human species to Angels of a kind. She heard their voices as they illuminated the Milky Way with their deific presence like the clean, fresh smell of babies. And she sang, "Hallelujah."

Abraxas paused to hear the deific voices singing from Tellus Mater too, and he couldn't be more proud. He had created man from cold matter on a cold world in a small system in a cold obscure arm of an average spiral galaxy. He had replicated his experiment with man on a hundred billion worlds in billions of galaxies though a multiverse shaped like a starfish. Most failed. They were killed by viruses or devoured by predators. They destroyed themselves with nuclear weapons. They were wiped out by plate tectonics or by the weather. They were driven to extinction by gamma ray bursts or by cometary, meteor, or planetary collision, or by their suns going nova. And they were destroyed by technologically superior but viciously savage aliens.

Ariel was the first of God's cold human creatures to become god of a kind. And the children of the Daughters and the Sons were the first to become Angels of a kind.

"See, Diana," he said. "See what they have become."

The Mother of Creation looked at her longtime companion. He was red in the face with exuberance and had to sit down. He was beside himself and in tears, filled with intense joy over a thing long wished for but never attained until now.

"One lowly creature becoming god," cried Abraxas, "makes it all worthwhile. And the rest have become Angels. Is it not joyous?"

"Yes," said Flora, as she looked out into the multiverse and found Ariel, and Earth, and the progeny of the Daughters of Tellus Mater and the Sons of Mars. She saw their deific radiance. She heard their beautiful voices. And she was moved to tears herself. "You were right," she said, "and I beg forgiveness."

Abraxas had been right all along to try his experiments with cold life across the multiverse. Like salmon fighting to return home, fighting against the odds, the humans of Earth had endured unimaginable hardships, but they had survived and evolved. Ariel was the first creature in the multiverse to become god of a kind. The others were the first to become Angels. They were nascent creatures and weak compared to her, but they had crossed over nevertheless. They were deities. And she marveled at their becoming.

Like the joy that filled the hearts of the Daughters of Tellus Mater when they received the first radio transmission from another world,

Flora's heart was filled with joy too, as was every heart in the Chorus, because, at long last, they knew that they were not alone.

Chapter 25 - duty

Ariel sat within the confines of her deific sanctuary on Tellus Mater for five billion years and communicated with the creatures of the seventh universe via the aerial system constructed on every habitable world. And no one ever said that god doesn't exist or wasn't listening. She answered every prayer. She appeared where she was needed. And she manifested herself, as only she could, in a trillion polymorphous perceptions of god, because she discovered near the beginning of her tenure that it was wisest to appear before the creatures in her realm in their form. She cared for the creatures of the seventh universe as a mother loves her children. And she was loved by them as mother god.

When it was time, just before the yellow dwarf star named Sol swelled to a red giant and engulfed the rocky inner planets of its system, including Tellus Mater, Ariel established an extradimensional realm and moved Haven to it. And within her own version of the Mandala Room of Heaven, she placed the seventh universe, and governed the Little Kingdom from there.

During Ariel's tenure, she journeyed in her mind across the vastness of the expanding seventh universe and reseeded worlds that had been seeded by God Almighty initially but had met with planetary disaster in the interim. With a deific thought, she reset the atmospheres on those worlds back to their ammonia-methane beginnings. Her rarefied thoughts sparked lightning in the atmospheres. And blobs of brown protein fell from the sky and seeded the primordial seas with the building blocks of life.

Ariel danced and life arose from every deific footfall, gaze, and touch. She was the farmer in the sky. She was Diana walking naked amid the lime green shoots and tendrils of the vine rows of Heaven.

She was the serpent Quetzalcoatl adorned in feathers of cerulean and lime. She was fertility itself. And as she spun round and around, life rippled out from her to the farthest reaches of the gossamer expanse that was her duty and privilege to steward. Life germinated, grew, and flowered everywhere. And it was glorious.

But corporeal life was terrified of death. The fear that plagued them bordered on an obsession, particularly with the ones who knew and knew they knew. It was the nature of their worlds that made them that way. It was kill or be killed. It was run faster, climb higher, and be vigilant. And Ariel was immensely disturbed by their obsession with death because it got in the way of them living their lives.

Ironically, she knew that there would come a time when she too would become obsessed with death. Only then would she realize that she had been created for that exact purpose. It had always been the destiny of human beings to evolve into gods of a kind. It had always been her destiny to become god of the seventh universe under Heaven. And it had always been Diana's plan to have Ariel administer a merciful death to Father, Son, and Holy Ghost, and to end everything, when the time was right, on that future day of days.

But when that day of days arrived, Ariel was unprepared. One deific day like any other, when the seventh universe was ancient and composed mostly of burned out cinders that could no longer regenerate, Ariel heard a whisper. She stared down the length of the Little Kingdom, in and out of space and time from the Big Bang to the Big Crunch, as if the gossamer expanse strewn with a trillion galaxies was a dark cave filled with Black Widow spider silk and riddled with ensnared white flies. And she heard something that was amiss. Amid the radio cacophony of her universe, beyond the crackle of sparks generated by the grinding collisions of rocky asteroids, beyond the chirping of gas giants, the flutters of pulsars, and the piercing hammer rings of solid crystalline iron neutron stars, and beyond the background cosmic static itself, she heard voices. And the voices whispered her name.

The chorus of whispers came from everywhere and from nowhere. And they spoke to her in one voice because they were of one mind, of one disembodied, scattered, and supposedly annihilated mind. And Ariel sensed that the scattered mind was an ancient entity bearing a perpetual punishment doled out long ago for a perfidy committed and destined.

And Ariel asked the scattered mind a question because she was curious and had to be sure. She asked every part of the seventh universe simultaneously. The nascent god asked the ancient entity, "Who are you?"

And from the farthest reaches of oblivion, the scattered liquid hydrogen condensate with a consciousness that refused to die responded to a question as old as time itself. From the brink of perpetual doom, from the razor's edge of eternity where creation's simplest atom ceased rotation, translation, and vibration, microscopic clumps of the supercold liquid that had been a complex soul once … quivered. And the diverse parts that made up the whole said: "I am he who is hated that once was she who was loved."

"Stand before me," ordered Ariel, "so I may gaze upon you."

And so, by god's command, the creature that existed in and out of time and in no place and in all places as disembodied and dislocated liquid packets that used to be a soul were heated by Ariel's rarefied thoughts and coalesced before her, at the speed of deific thought, from everywhere and nowhere, into a coherent entity once more.

The creature returned to full consciousness in the midst of seemingly falling from a great height. It appeared before Ariel initially as a sphere of intense light brighter than the sun, brighter than Elektra when she once glowed before the throne of God Almighty. And Ariel recognized the creature as the twin sister of Hephzibah of Heaven before Sheba was goddess of Tellus Mater, and akin to her friend, Seraph, and devoted servant Elektra who had passed on.

As Ariel gazed upon her visitor, its appearance changed as per God Almighty's edict written so long ago. But in the midst of its metamorphosis from a female Angel of the highest order into something male and utterly hideous, Ariel exerted her deific influence and reclaimed its soul. She did what Heaven refused to do because of a destiny written long ago in *God's Great Book*.

The God of the seventh universe forgave the damaged, discarded, and fallen entity. And in so doing, Ariel snatched her from ignominy and re-established her as an Angel of Angels. Hephaestia, in all of her fiery-orange majesty with three pairs of pristine seraphic wings opened wide, floated before the new god. And the sight of the restored Seraph was glorious to behold.

"I thank you," said Hephaestia, as she examined her beautiful long fingernails. "It has been a seeming eternity since I was so perfect."

"You are far from perfect," said Ariel. "Not even I am perfect. And I am god of this Little Kingdom. You are merely released from the punishment inflicted upon you so long ago. I relieve you of the burden, the curse, and the destiny once written for you. I forgive you. Your slate is wiped clean. It is up to you whether you shall ever forgive those who imposed this destiny upon you and whether you can forgive yourself."

"You are a god unknown to me," said the cleansed anathema. "I see that you are called Ariel and have been adopted by my Mother and dubbed Nemorensis. That is a rare privilege. I am envious."

"I have not spoken to the Father or the Mother in a very long time," said Ariel.

The Seraph closed its eyes and sensed the parameters of the seventh universe in all of its eleven dimensions, and said, "I can see that. You are fiercely independent. You and I are alike in that regard. You have come a long way and done well for yourself daughter of Atom and Eva. I was there, you know, in the Garden with them in the beginning."

"I know."

The Seraph sighed. "Of course you do … you are god here. You have some of the Father and the Mother in you. But you have some of me in you, as well. How could you not? You are the progeny of my corruption. We are all manifestations of a greater whole. So, to what do I owe this honor? Why have you snatched me from the obscurity of oblivion? When Hephzibah finds out that I have been reclaimed, my one-time twin sister will defecate demons."

"It has always been my destiny to bring you back at this time," said Ariel, "to embrace you, and to forgive you, if only to be mildly corrupted by your hatred so I may steel myself for the inevitable task that I must eventually perform. Look into my mind."

Hephaestia looked into the mind of god and saw the disintegration of Heaven.

"You intend to complete what I started so long ago," said Hephaestia. "You plan to destroy Paradise, and to kill the Father. Are you that powerful?"

"I shall be," said Ariel.

"Yes," Hephaestia shouted exuberantly. "There is a god. Hallelujah. We are alike, you and me."

Ariel shook her head.

164

"No," she said, "we are not. You would take pleasure from the destruction of Heaven and from the murder of God Almighty; whereas, I do not. You would exert your freedom of choice to subsume order with chaos because you are egocentric, because it is still all about you; whereas, I shall perform my altruistic and dolorous duty because it is necessary. You would destroy Heaven and kill God as an act of hatred; whereas, I will do it as an act of kindness. You have clearly learned nothing after an eternity of solitude; whereas, even in the first few moments of my existence as god, I could see that it wasn't about me. Although I have purged that part of you created by the Father to instigate the War of Heaven, you continue to be corrupt because you choose to be. And because you continue to be a dark Angel by choice alone, I too shall dispense with you. It was a mistake to reconstitute you. But unlike your twin sister, who could not dispatch you utterly because she loved you despite your selfishness and viciousness, I shall not disperse you amid the galaxies of my universe as she did. I shall dispense with you totally and utterly."

"You can try, foolish young god," said Hephaestia. "But you forget that you have restored me to my full powers. I shall resist you. And perhaps I shall even kill you, and rei   The nascent god smiled at the ancient Seraph, and said, "A firefly streaking across a garden, at midnight, cannot conceive of the garden in the midday sun, let alone she who planned it, planted it, and presides over it."

And so, with a thought, Ariel flung Hephaestia into the cobalt blue boson and fermion plasma of the Celestial Sea from which all things come and inevitably go. The Seraph dissolved to elementary particles. And that was that. All that remained of her was a small but necessary stain on Ariel's soul.

Soon after, the burned out seventh universe ran its course, folded back upon itself, and formed an Alpha crystal once more awaiting the Word of God. And Ariel was struck with déjà vu because the day of days that she had dreaded for an eternity was finally upon her. She knew what she must do. It was time for the prodigal daughter to return to Heaven. It was time for Ariel Nemorensis the god of the seventh universe to play her final scene in the deific drama, and to confront her destiny.

Chapter 26 - terminus

Ariel journeyed to Heaven initially with Athena and Elektra. And she fully expected to return with her friends one day. But when that day of days finally came, Ariel traveled alone. The god of the seventh universe, the Tellusian Angel, and the Seraph were supposed to be eternal. At least, that was what Ariel believed at the outset of her tenure as god. But, as she discovered, even eternity has a limit. And, in due course, they all succumbed to the ravages of time. Ariel lasted longest because she was youngest, but was noticeably older. Angelic Athena departed first. But, in a deific sense, no spirit ever really dies. Elektra of the Seraphim departed later. So, when the aged god of the seventh universe finally returned to Paradise, she journeyed alone. And she discovered that Heaven was older too. It was no longer the Kingdom of God that she journeyed to initially. It was ancient, neglected, and in ruins. All but the highest Angels had returned to the cobalt blue Celestial Sea from which all things come. Heaven had become a ghost town and a graveyard. And the deities that remained were diminished.

It was in her Manichean nature to travel to a vibrant Heaven initially as Eros the god of life, exuberant, fresh, and young. But she returned to a diminished Heaven as Thanatos the god of death because there was need for such a thing. She came once as serene Quetzalcoatl adorned in parrot feathers of cerulean and lime with her body stained aquamarine and cobalt blue like the Celestial Sea from which all things come. But she returned as crazed Tezcatlipoca adorned in the pyramid headdress and crow feathers of a Mayan high priest with her eyes painted midnight black and her body stained with the fiery-orange flames of destruction. She was a deific serpent with six pairs of wings.

She was a sphere of light brighter and hotter than the entire seventh universe. She was the end.

It had always been Ariel's destiny to bring the end to all things. Only a one-time Daughter of Tellus Mater who had never known a male could do such a thing. Only a virgin god devoid of a soul mate would have the strength of will required to perform the horrific task.

Ariel had been god of the seventh universe and, as such, had cared for the creatures within her domain. And, in and of itself, her caring was love of a kind. Hers was the love of a mother for her children. It was the love of a caretaker. It was the love of a steward at best. At the outset, her love was authoritarian and obsessive. But as her children changed, evolved or perished, she stepped back from her commitment. Life in the seventh universe came and went and returned and vanished again many times during her tenure. And each time life went and came crawling back she abandoned the creatures within her domain a little more.

Only someone who had never known the ecstasy of a lover and the pained, panged heartache of that love lost could be so cold and pragmatic, and bring an end to everything. Only Ariel could dissolve Heaven because when she looked at the Mother and Father, at Adonai and Sheba, and at Gabriel and Rebecca she did not comprehend their special love. She understood intellectually that they were mated pairs. She understood the workings of pheromone stimulated carnal sexual attraction although she had never experienced it herself when she was Tellusian. But she was utterly oblivious to the emotional commitment that went with it. And it was hard enough for her to understand the cool, pitiful, abstract notion of human love let alone the solar passion which enflamed the hearts of the Angels and the Gods of Heaven. The shortcoming was her deific flaw. Virginity was her deific strength.

Ariel passed through the fiery-orange curtain of Heaven within which once flew creatures of energy, fire, and mind. But they were no more. And she stepped out the other side, without challenge, into Paradise. She kneeled, out of profound respect, upon the golden floor of Heaven, but no God was there to greet her. The Father, Son, and Holy Host had not sensed her coming. Neither were there any sentries from the Chorus, on patrol.

Ariel had once assumed that the realm of fire and light was eternal, that God was eternal, that she was eternal. She was wrong. Just as she had grown older, and the seventh universe had run its course and had folded back upon itself, Heaven with its Gods and Chorus had grown older too. Because she was the newcomer at the dance, she showed the least signs of aging. But they had all aged, and the Father and Mother were in the last stage of their deific lives before the inevitable end.

Heaven, as the external projection of their extralucent minds, made their conditions obvious for all to see, for the Mother of Creation and God Almighty had become senile and one could barely help herself let alone the other.

When Ariel first visited, Heaven was orderly. It was the physical manifestation of the order in God's mind. But his mind was now chaotic. Things that had to be done were left undone and were quickly forgotten. Choices were left undecided because God had lost the ability to choose. Diana was no longer recognized as creator, companion, and spouse. In fact, when Abraxas looked upon himself in a mirror, he could no longer comprehend who he was. He no longer recalled his name nor did he remember how to find his way home to the Citadel, to his throne room, or to his private chambers.

Abraxas would sometimes walk the streets of Heaven for days before he was missed, and the Mother sent out Angels to find him, and to escort him back. He swore that everyone who spoke with him, or smiled at him, or tried to help him was a stranger out to steal from him. And when he became agitated, he reverted to the language of the ancients who resided in the Odeon of Heaven, but were long gone by then. And what the Angels heard was gibberish.

Of all the sad things that Hephzibah had seen during her travails and travels, and had commented on as Seraph and as Goddess, the sight of her weakened Father was beyond emotions. Once she cried readily. Now she could no longer weep. She only stared at Abraxas when he failed to recognize her as his daughter or when he mistook her fiery-orange hair for the fiery-orange hair of the Mother of Creation, as Diana used to look when she was young. Hephzibah held back her tears. The Mother taught her that much. For if she let go, if she began to weep, she wasn't sure she would ever stop.

When Ariel first visited Heaven, it seemed perfect. The streets were filled with Angels. The vineyards were lush. The fields overflowed with bounty. Now, the population was sparse. The vineyards were dry and cracked. And the fields were burned. Heaven seemed perfect still, for the most part, for how else would it seem? But Ariel could discern the ever so slight patina upon its perfect polish, the merest green stain upon its perfect sash that put the rest of reality to shame.

Ariel had seen beyond Father, Mother, and herself. And what she saw did not disturb her, although it was unsettling to Abraxas to see one of his cold creatures grown to god now greater than him. But his perceptions were skewed because he was diminished. It was an outcome he had not foreseen or written about in his *Great Book*. Typical of him in his condition, he got flustered and red in the face, and had to be calmed and distracted by the Mother.

Ariel had expected a celebration upon her return to Heaven. But there was none. So, while they had tea and shortbread cookies, she told Abraxas and Diana about her exploits since they first met. And the elderly manifestations of God nodded agreeably, as old folks do.

Ariel explained to Father and Mother what she had done with the seventh universe. She told them that she had disintegrated the evil in it, brought order to it, communicated with the inhabitants everywhere through a vast communication system, and done some good overall. But she also explained to the deities that it always amounted to the same thing: god and subjects, a great divide in beings that, at first, was satisfying to her because of the concept of *noblesse oblige* and stewardship, but eventually became nothing more than sycophancy on their part and narcissism on hers. She explained that she had become sick of the relationship long before the universe burned itself out. But it was something that the Mother already knew and had already experienced herself.

Ariel talked to them about her disappointment in herself, and the deep, abiding depression that followed. She had wanted to do more. She had wanted to be better.

"Did you do the best you could," asked Diana.

"It wasn't enough," cried the young god.

"Did you play at being God to merely satisfy yourself?"

"I did it for them," cried Ariel. "I did it all for them. They were my children."

And when the Mother looked within Ariel's mind she saw that it was so. From the smallest virons to the largest cetaceans, Ariel existed for them.

"Then you have done well, my child," said the Mother.

While she spoke, Abraxas absent-mindedly and annoyingly fumbled with the two sphere fob attached by a golden ring to the golden keys of

170

Heaven. Once upon a time, he realized that the spheres were two very real planets. But now he was too far gone to see that the biofilm on the spheres was actually intelligent life, and his nervous fumbling was subjecting that life to disaster on a planetary scale. He was subjecting them to repeated collision, planetary scale electrostatic discharge amounting to super-lightning, tectonic displacement, subduction, tsunamis, and volcanism. So, while the Mother distracted him, Ariel liberated the key-chain from Abraxas and put the poor tortured creatures of the devastated worlds out of their misery. She tossed the keys of Heaven, with their golden ring, and the dual planetary fob into the cobalt blue Celestial Sea from which all things come and eventually go.

Then Ariel Nemorensis presented Diana of the Groves with the Alpha Crystal that was the seventh universe. Within it was a wispy web of dark matter. And hanging upon that cosmic gossamer, like the corpses of whiteflies snagged in the gauzy filaments of a Black Widow spider web, were billions of galaxies grouped in clusters. Within those galaxies were the corpses of trillions of stars, every star that had ever burned, every red giant or white dwarf, every supernova, nebula, miniscule neutron star, and colossal black hole, every brown sun, gas giant, and small rocky moon and world. The gossamer expanse once burned brightly and illuminated the cosmic night. Now its stars were reduced to coals. Its heat was lost. It was dark and dead. And the Alpha Crystal was black.

The Daughters of Tellus Mater and the Sons of Mars were there too within the crystal. The Gabrielican sisters of Atonement and their Uteran symbiotes metamorphosed through extreme sacrifice into Angels were there. Beside them were Daffodil, Thorn, and Ariel's mother Helen who were incinerated in the Rancorian nuclear attack that transformed a Tellusian farm girl into god, and would inadvertently transform an obscure pale blue dot in the Sol system, near the inner rim of the Orion Arm, in the Gould Belt, within the rarified supernova remnant of Geminga, into the center of the seventh universe.

The seventh universe had all been created by God out of rarefied proton ether. And from that ether everything unfolded over its natural course until it was spent. Now, the seventh universe was no more. It had folded back upon itself in a Big Crunch and compressed, and was ready, once again, for the next Big Bang that could only be initiated by the Hand of God.

Tellusian Seed by Mark Carter

And so, Ariel placed the Alpha Chrystal, like a large black diamond full of star stuff, upon Diana's outstretched and open right palm. And the god of the seventh universe said to the God of Creation, "Thank you, Mother. It has taught me much."

"And what have you learned, my darling?"

"I have learned," said Ariel, "that everyone and everything has a destiny whether or not it is written in *God's Great Book*."

The Mother of Creation laughed, and Ariel sighed.

"And what is your destiny?" asked Diana.

"See what I see," said Ariel.

The Mother looked within Ariel's extralucent mind and witnessed the collapse of the multiverse shaped like a starfish in the Mandala Room of Heaven. She witnessed the collapse of Heaven itself. And she witnessed the dissolution of Hephzibah, Adonai, Abraxas, Ariel, and herself. She witnessed the dissolution and the compression of everything into a packet of antimatter, a veritable God particle, floating in the oblivion of the cobalt blue Celestial Sea beyond space and time or existence itself.

"And why," asked Diana Nemorensis, the Mother of Creation, "would you do such a thing?"

"Because," said Ariel, "it is time. And you cannot, in your condition, and by your very nature, do it yourself."

Diana blinked because it was true. In that moment, she realized that Abraxas and the others had degraded so far that Ariel was now greater than any of them, greater than even her. She realized that the young god had returned to Heaven to dispatch them mercifully, something she had neither the strength nor the will to do herself. And she was relieved.

Every bell in Heaven began to ring because the end was nigh. And Ariel began to sing a nursery rhyme handed down to her in the Tellusian verbal tradition and as old as time itself, from a land called England on the old Earth destroyed by collision with Lucifer. She had learned the rhyme when she was a girl in pig-tails, on a farm, in the heat of a dry summer.

Oranges and lemons,
Say the bells of St. Clement's.

The Mother of Creation summoned Abraxas, Adonai and Hephzibah to her side. She told them that she loved them. And they told her that they loved her. She explained to them what was about to happen and they were alarmed, then defensive. But she placed her right palm upon their hearts to quiet their tormented souls. She told them that it was time, that it was the end of the cycle of their existence. She told them that it was natural.

> You owe us five farthings,
> Say the bells of St. Martin's.

Adonai told her that he was frightened, that he didn't want to die again, not for the third time, not forever. And in a calm, quiet voice, Flora said, "Nothing is forever, my beautiful boy, not for us, not for any of us."

> When will you pay me?
> Say the bells of Old Bailey.

Abraxas was also frightened although he didn't say as much, and wasn't sure why. But she could see it in his face.

With a thought, Diana made him lucid for a few fleeting moments.

"I shall miss you, beloved," he said to her in a voice that quavered. "You have been the be-all of my existence, my constant companion, my friend, and my lover. I do not know what I shall do without you. I would like to think that a great love such as ours is eternal."

"I believe it is, beloved," she said, as she stroked his bearded jaw tenderly.

> When I grow rich,
> Say the bells of Shoreditch.

"I too am affected by all of this, Mother," said Hephzibah, "but not by thoughts of oblivion. I am stuck by the great sadness of it all, by the waste, by the solitude that each of us will suffer, and that I shall suffer once again."

"Do not be sad," said Diana Nemorensis to the onetime goddess of Tellus Mater from which sprang the new god that doomed them all. "Rejoice, for none of us shall be alone. Rest assured. Rejoice, for the complete and utter end of this cycle of existence will bring forth new reality. Rejoice, for reality hates a vacuum. Moreover, reality hates waste. Our time is at an end, as all creatures, stars, galaxies, and universes have a time in which they flourish and eventually terminate. Now is our time to be no more. But we shall see each other again. Believe and it shall be so. I bestow my eternal blessing upon you, my precious daughter, and upon you all."

When will that be?
Say the bells of Stepney.

Diana turned her attention back to Ariel, and said, "There are three small voices you must hear, and one last thing that I must do before all is said and done."

"As you wish," said Ariel respectfully.

And so, Gabriel and Rebecca who had been taken by Angels from their lives on the old Earth so long ago, and Shepherd who had been crucified on the New Earth four million years later, were released from the Tree of Diana where they had been kept safe by the Mother of Creation for an eternity. And they were permitted to speak because they were special, and it was time.

The three human beings got down upon knees that cracked because they were ancient in years beyond all expectation. And with bowed heads they too spoke to Ariel.

And Gabriel, author of the *Book of Gabriel* carried to the stars of the Milky Way galaxy by the Gabrielican Sisters of Atonement so long ago, said, "Help us, Ariel. I beg you. We are old and cannot help ourselves."

"Help us, dearest Ariel," begged Rebecca. "Show us and them your mercy."

And Shepherd spoke too, he who had been crucified on the Bloodwood and resurrected, and who the Mother had taken unto her bosom, said, "I too beg you to help us, divine one, and to help them most of all. Help those Gods and Angels whom we love here in Heaven that have become so old they cannot help themselves. I beg you on our behalf and on theirs, on this day of days, to assist us all in the inevitable. It is not the thought of dying that terrifies me. It is the sensation of transition. Please, I beg you. Make it fast."

174

Chapter 26 - terminus

I do not know,
Says the great bell of Bow.

Thanatos looked once again upon Diana of the Groves.

The ancient God bowed her head respectfully before the young god, and said, "Thank you for your patience. You do us a great service. But before you commence your dolorous duty, I want you to know that we forgive you."

Ariel bit her lip to force back tears. "From God's mouth to god's ear," she said.

Then, before Diana had a chance to change her mind, the Manichean god that Ariel was performed her unspoken and unwritten destiny. Thanatos assisted the Gods in Heaven with their demise. The savageries of eternity had already robbed them of their deific dignity. They were feeble and infirm. They lacked control of their bodily functions, and were senile.

Ariel raised her right hand over her head, like a Mayan high priest from ancient Earth, and dissolved the exquisitely beautiful equations that held reality together and took God so long to create. And in the stillness of the Mandala Room of Heaven, upon the colored sand that defined the eight arms of the multiverse shaped like a starfish, matter ceased telling space how to curve and space ceased telling matter how to move. Black holes collided. Space and time undulated like discordant waves on a tumultuous sea. Tendrexes and vortexes annihilated. And the multiverse ceased to exist.

With her left hand, Ariel raised a sharp dagger chipped from volcanic glass over her head, a smoking obsidian dagger, a Mayan sacrificial dagger, and dissolved Gabriel and Rachel, Shepherd, the Chorus of Angels, Adi and Sheba.

Then Ariel dissolved the Lord of Song by speaking his true name. And there was a blaze of light in every word.

Alpha
Abraxas rex
Elohim
El-Olam
El Shaddai
Omega

What his name meant was: I am the Beginning and the End, King Abraxas, God, God of Everlasting Time, God Almighty.

Thunder rumbled. Heaven shook. And Angel Falls poured from Ariel's eyes.

"Hallelujah," cried Ariel. "Hallelujah," cried Thanatos. "Hallelujah," cried Tezcatlipoca.

> Here comes a candle
> to light you to bed,
> And here comes a chopper
> to chop off your head.

In so saying, Tezcatlipoca plunged the black, chipped, glass dagger that she held in her sinister hand into God's chest, and cut out his heart. The shock wave of her sweet brutality rushed out over reality, like a ripple expanding from a pebble thrown into the calm center of a dark pool, and whispered the name Judas. And God Almighty ceased to exist.

Then Ariel dissolved the woven fabric of Heaven into the chaos of the cobalt blue Celestial Sea from which all things come. And because destruction is easier and much faster than creation, everything collapsed quickly upon itself. And Paradise ceased to exist.

Ariel kissed Diana on the lips tenderly, and said, "All good things must come to an end. All God things must come to an end. Hold me in your arms, Mother, for even I am afraid."

"Do not be frightened, sweetheart," said Diana Nemorensis, "for I am here." So saying, Diana of the Groves, the last holdout and first among the Gods, upon witnessing the dissolution of everything, joined hands with Ariel. And together, like friends jumping off a cliff at the local quarry into the cool water below on a hot, summer day, they dissolved out of existence together in one, surreal, and united leap of faith.

And the Celestial Sea became as blood.

Then, with all of it gone, with all of them gone, reality compressed to a single point, circled and fizzled for three complete counterclockwise revolutions through the scarlet void that the Celestial Sea had become, and finally winked out of existence.

And as Hephzibah had foreseen, it was all so sad, but there was nobody left to shed a tear.

Chapter 27 - regenesis

Seemingly forever beyond her apparent demise, beyond space and time itself which no longer existed, amid the black desolation and utter solitude of the eternal night, oblivion, and void, a primordial consciousness became self-aware. She was elemental, formless, and inert, and existed inside herself, within a spherical bubble where every direction was up. She saw herself even though she had no eyes with which to see. And she heard herself even though she had no ears with which to hear. Her first sensation was nausea, the initial, unspecified pain of consciousness. But her first instinctive thought was fear, the fear of existence, the fear of transition from something undefined to other. And so, she cried out into the nothingness, but she had no mouth with which to scream.

Because the only direction was up, she arose, and surfaced in the form of a flickering flame who could not, should not, would not die upon the moonless, inky, Celestial Sea at midnight. And this ephemeral creature whose deific day lasted an eternity dreamed that she was the One. And the One was God. And her flame stained the Celestial Sea fiery-orange.

Amid the fiery-orange Celestial Sea of Strings, God wrote the mathematics for the elementary particles of force and matter that would define reality. She imagined protonic ether from which to construct an ethereal being. And with an extralucent thought she molded her initial, default form into the shape of an exquisite human female, elegant, lithe, and tall with long, jet black hair that fell to the small of her back. If the times had been other and the location ancient Greece, she could easily have been mistaken for a vestal virgin from the Oracle of Delphi or perhaps Aphrodite herself.

She ran her fingertips over the beautiful nakedness of her arms and legs, her hands and feet, her body, and her face, and was pleased with her own re-creation.

And she rode the fiery-orange Celestial Sea upon a half shell, and stepped ashore upon a new Heaven freshly thought into existence.

And she said, "I am that I am." And her words, the Word of God regenerated, thundered across the face of Heaven, as once long ago they had thundered before Moses on Mount Horeb, on an obscure planet called Earth, orbiting a yellow dwarf star named Sol, in a remote galaxy called the Milky Way, in the seventh arm of the multiverse shaped like a starfish, in the ancient Mandala Room of Heaven.

I am the God of Creation.
I am the One and true God resurrected.
I am perfection perfected.

Then the Great I Am spoke her name, and thundered, "Alpha, Omega, Elohim Infinitum, Diana Nemorensis." And there was lightning in every letter of her name. And Heaven trembled for her name was the Word. And the Word was God. And what her name meant was I am the Beginning and the End. I am Eternal God. I am Queen Diana of the Groves. And every atom of reality trembled at the magnificence of her name, and sang her praises. Even the rocks and stones upon the shore of the fiery-orange Celestial Sea sang, "Hallelujah. Hosanna in the highest for God who was, is, and shall be has come again."

She had come and gone. She was here again but would eventually go once more. Reality would end. And then, like now, she would burst into existence with a Word and the entire grand cycle with a story and a destiny of its own would occur again like variations on a musical theme, like a sine wave following another, like the ebb and flow of the tides until the heat death of the Celestial Sea itself when too little energy remained for the Word to resurrect anything. On that day, in some distant, unimaginable deific future, the dark fabric of reality would moan its agony, like the sad, tormented songs of Humpback whales on moonless nights weeping into a Sea of Bitterness over the future, imagined death of God. And a deific era of life would be subsumed by the bleak horrific nothingness of the perpetual darkness and the eternal abyss.

But that unimaginable time was not now, and would not occur for a deific eternity. Now was the time of great beginning. Diana existed again. She had re-imagined Heaven back into being. Soon she would re-imagine Abraxas, Adonai, Hephzibah and her sisters, and the Angelic Chorus back into being, as well, with changes. And she would re-imagine Ariel back into being too, and add her to the pantheon of Heaven. It was only right. The human race deified in Ariel had earned the privilege of a place in Heaven among the gods. But, for now, Diana's attention was drawn to a nascent multiverse shaped like a starfish freshly created within the new Mandala Room of Heaven. It was hers to watch over and to nurture. This time, she would do it right.

Diana imagined a matrix of alternating S and Z twists of silk crêpe and covered herself with a lustrous, sheer, fiery-orange, chiffon chiton and himation of ancient Greek design. And she thought fiery-orange chiffon sandals upon her feet.

Upon the open palm of her right hand, Diana of the Groves who was the Mother of Creation and the Master Architect of the multiverse cradled a pale blue egg, a robin's egg. It was the representation of reality in one small package. She blessed the egg and threw it from Heaven out over and beyond the fiery-orange Celestial Sea from which she came.

She cried out with all of the love a mother has for the life in her pregnant womb, "Let there be light."

And in a flash that shocked the perpetual night into day, she gave birth to everything.

In the nine arms of the re-imagined multiverse shaped like a starfish in the colored sand on the floor of the new Mandala Room of Heaven, the force of her divine will caused the Alpha particles to explode. And those Big Bangs burst their heated ingredients into the voids to form nine universes where previously there had been eight. There had been but one universe when she first incarnated. And a universe had been added each time she re-imagined herself. Now there were nine universes in a multiverse whose expanding, rarefied contents would eventually coalesce to form galaxies, stars, and planets.

When the multiverse had cooled sufficiently, her most fragile creation would emerge everywhere. Life, as she designed it in her extralucent imagination, as self-replicating sequences of proteins affixed to ascending and descending chains of ribose sugars, would spark into existence amid primordial seas of methane and ammonia. And it would evolve.

Hydrophilic phospholipid bilayers would form and separate extracellular from intracellular seas. Chlorophyll molecules would allow plants to convert sunlight and water into sugar. Copper centered hemocyanin and iron centered hemoglobin would arise from magnesium centered chlorophyll molecules and allow animals in the sea and on land to exchange carbon dioxide and oxygen too. And using the chloroplast template, it would allow retinal cones and rods containing rhodopsin to see.

And in its vast biodiversity, life would fly the air, swim the oceans, and walk the land on trillions of alien worlds. And all of it would be glorious.

Sentient beings would eventually understand that creation by intelligent design was behind everything, and that Diana was the designer. They would come to love and to respect life, and to love and to respect her as its architect. Eventually, these thinking creatures would travel into space seeking her. And they would find her.

What Diana imagined was all good. It would forever be nothing but good. In every sense of the word, it was an extension of her. Life, in all of its biodiversity and splendor, was God. And she was everywhere.

Diana danced in her elegant, fiery-orange, floating chiffon chiton as she had once danced with Abraxas when they were young and beautiful and hopeful.

One, two, three ... one, two, three
One, two, three ... one, two, three
One, two, three ... one, two, three
One, two, three ... one, two, three

She danced as Hephzibah had once danced in the wheat field of Paradise with Adonai before the War of Heaven when they were in love but had not yet professed it. She danced as she had danced, as they had danced, in celebration of life and love to the glorious three four tempo of a waltz.

Arms outstretched ... dance your best
One, two, three ... one, two, three
Blood rushing ... face flushing
One, two, three ... one, two, three

Spinning round … round, round, round
Heart, beat, beat … beat, beat, beat
Hand on hip … hand in hand
His heart hers … her heart his

One, two, three … one, two, three
Step, step, step … step, step, step
Spinning round … all around
Let there be light she thought

"Let there be light," she cried, for the second time, as afterbirth squeezed from the fountain of creation. "Let there be light."
And *Mirabile dictu, Mirabile visu,* scarlet stigmata burst from her feet, and hands, and head because creation was the greatest miracle, the greatest pain, and the greatest sacrifice of all.

Once again, it was day one.
And there was light.
And it was
God

about the author

MARK A. CARTER holds a B.A. in Drama and Psychology, a B.Ed., an Honors B.A. in English, and an M.A., with thesis, in English Language and Literature. He lives within sight of Heaven and Hell, in the outskirts of Canada, and in the shadow of so-called civilization, with his wife. He wrote *Tellusian Seed*, by hand, in the presence of Messengers, using his fabled translucent, red, fountain pen. He is also the author of *Hephzibah of Heaven* and *Thea of the Seraphim*.

afterword

What makes each day special for me is waking at four forty-five every
morning, putting on the coffee, opening the windows, and listening to
my local robin as it breaks the stillness of the early hour with its
morning song. The smell and sound of coffee bubbling, dripping, and
steaming and the mellow vocalizations of my fiery-orange breasted
friend delight my heart and soul, as they do my wife's, and remind us,
in the tranquility of the moment, amid a world perpetually twisted by
turmoil, that we are fortunate, and that God exists.

acknowledgments

As fate would have it, I finished the rewrite of *Tellusian Seed* and particularly Chapter 26 - *terminus* from bed 8111B at Windsor Regional Hospital Metropolitan Campus where I was a patient from Dec. 7 through Dec. 20, 2011.

If I was to muse philosophically, I would say that, after the thrashing I gave the Devil in *Hephzibah of Heaven* and in *Thea of the Seraphim,* and, to a lesser extent, in *Tellusian Seed*, the Dark Lord finally got his due, and took my right big toe. On a practical level, I was there because I was already compromised by diabetes and a Staph A infection got the better of me. But to muse theologically, I would say that I was there because God wanted to make a point.

God does not make mistakes. I fully believe that the entire misadventure with my infected toe was designed to get my attention. It was designed to get me into WRH-Met and to show me, since I see with better eyes than most, the error of my thinking. My opinion of mankind was, without a doubt, jaded when I wrote *Hephzibah of Heaven*. And that attitude has lingered. I believe that God, through his Messengers and through the humble bacteria that infected me, wanted me to see once again. He wanted to remind me that there are dedicated people who do great good in this world. I had forgotten. Even worse, I had become bitter. My world had become isolated and small. But now, I have been reminded. So, this experience is not about the destination. It isn't about the sacrifice of one great toe. It's about the journey. It's about balance and perspective. It's about seeing again. And I do.

There are so many people that I need to thank.

First and foremost, I would like to thank Niki Grady RN, Wound Care Nurse, Saint Elizabeth Health Care, for seeing the signs of my Cellulitis before anyone else, and for ringing the alarm bell so others would notice.

I would like to thank the following people at Windsor Regional Hospital Metropolitan Campus who helped me through my ordeal: Dr. Raphael Cheung, my Endocrinologist, jogger, and sweet man who, with his corny jokes, open heart, and kind soul raised my spirits at the outset of my hospital stay, gave me perspective, and kept me going; Dr. David Seski, Internal Medicine, a sweet, soft spoken man with a kind soul who shared a generous amount of his time with me to allay my fears, and to inform me that my condition would get worse before it got better; Dr. Corinna Quan, Infectious Diseases, Tecumseh Rd. Byng Clinic, a small package with an infectious smile containing a great mind, for the behind the scenes work she did to identify my bacterial infection; Dr. Saulivs John Kizis, Family Medicine, *call me Sal*, a sweet, soft spoken man with a kind soul who watched over me as he flew past, with caduceus in hand, on the winged sandals of Hermes; Dr. Joseph Shaban, Endocrinologist, dapper dresser, gushing science fiction aficionado, and sweet guy for being my Angel standing guard over my diabetic numbers before, during, and after surgery; Dr. Samia Ghali, Radiologist, Nuclear Medicine, a stoic Egyptian Physician with a kind heart, for confirming that my infection was restricted solely to my right big toe; Eleanor Bardgett, RN, MClSc, Enterostomal Therapist, wound care nurse, a.k.a. *the puss queen* for her gentle touch, her bag of tricks, and her quiet wit; the four mushrooms of the X-Ray Department Special Procedures Room where my Peripherally Inserted Central Catheter was installed by Dr. Fareed Denath, Radiologist, a gentle man with quiet wit and interesting stories: Lisa Greenwood, X-Ray Technologist, Lisa Skieneh, X-Ray Technologist, *you have to mention us*, Lisa Smith, X-Ray Technologist, and Rosie Simmons, X-Ray Technologist, with special thanks to two other mushrooms: Sonja Serafimovski, X-Ray Technologist, *poster girl and princess*, and Geri Thrasher, Lead X-Ray technologist, *the old hat*, and *dinosaur of the Department*; the girls of Nuclear Medicine: Michele (*with one L)* B., Senior Nuclear Medicine Technologist, for listening to my worries and for giving me precious words of encouragement; Lucy B., Nuclear Medicine Technologist, *smile Lucy*; Jean C., Nuclear Medicine Technologist, who I must apologize to for abandoning my wheelchair

186

after 5 and journeying up to 8 North on my own; Caroline C., Nuclear Medicine Technologist, for ever so sweetly removing blood from my tortured veins, extracting and irradiating my white blood cells, and injecting them back into me so that the extent of my infection could be mapped; and Sandy K., Nuclear Medicine Technologist, *Don't call me ma'am.*

A special place in my heart is reserved for Cheryl McLaughlin, X-Ray Porter and 30 year veteran, for her jovial disposition; Jules St. Martin, X-Ray Porter, exuberant personality and great guy, for the Patch Adams like shirts he wears to brighten the days of the patients he transports; Hugh Robson, RPN, transfer nurse, a deeply protective man with a goofy laugh who was the guardian of my medical pedigree and the Angel who watched over me on the journey from WRH-Met to Hotel-Dieu Grace Hospital for surgery; and, Gerri Carey, RPN, transfer nurse, Grand Bend girl, free spirit, and a force of nature unto herself, for seeing me safely back to WRH-Met after surgery at Hotel-Dieu Grace Hospital, and for giving me a big hug a week later when I finally left for home.

I would like to thank Alex, RN, in Emergency for her tenderness when I arrived by ambulance and was half out of my mind with fever.

I would like to thank the young nurses on 4 West who treated me like gold when I was at my most pathetic and vulnerable: Amy, RN, Hanna, RN, Istar (Izzy) Dahir, RN, and Mike, RN, and their Unit Manager Colette Clarke, RN, MScN, who, on two occasions, took all of the time in the world to speak with me.

I would also like to thank the nurses of 8 North who treated me with tender, loving care: Katie L., RN; Brenda M., RN who washed my back; Branka P., RN, a Serbian darling whose name means *glorious defender*; Nevis S. A., RN, whose name means *snow*; Tatiana I, RN, my caring and enthusiastic friend from Ukraine; Tanya, RN; Denise B., RN who showed me great kindness; Linda Y., RN, *wonder girl*; Trisha A., RN, a straight shooter who usually works on 5; Michelle B., RN, who looked after me like a caring mother with superwoman zeal looking after her own child; and, Shari C., RN, a sweet lady so suited to the profession of nursing that she glides on the breeze, and who counted my toes at the post-op unveiling of my right foot to make sure that only my big toe had been taken.

I would also like to thank Megan, RN, BSc, Housekeeper - 4 West, who hopes to one day be hired as a nurse, who stopped to talk with me for a few moments when I desperately needed to talk with someone; Terri-Lynn R., the Ride-On Automatic Scrubber pilot who kept my hallway on 8 North clean, and always had a smile for me; Linda P., Housekeeper, who daily dumped my trash and washed the floor around and beneath my bed at 8111B, and always shared a kind word; Brenda Girard, Carbolizer, one of the dirtiest and most hazardous jobs in the hospital, for her words of encouragement, *Don't cry or you'll make me cry too*; the girls of *At Your Request Room Service Dining* who took my orders: Darlene D., Laura K., Linda J., Melissa T., Nina T., Ruth F., and Susan G, and the kind people who delivered meals to my bedside and collected my trays when I was finished; and Rocky Hebert of Care Medical Transportation Services for delivering me with TLC. You are all so appreciated.

Before I move on, I would like to thank David Mark Musyj, President and CEO of Windsor Regional Hospital for the ethos of *Outstanding Care – No Exceptions* that percolates his fine institution and the people who work there.

And I would like to extend a very special thank you to Dr. Carman M. Iannicello, Vascular Surgeon, master craftsman and humble *doer* at Hotel-Dieu Grace Hospital, for squeezing me into his busy schedule on the last day of surgery before Christmas, and for amputating the diseased spring roll that my right big toe had become after the relentless tunneling of *Staphylococcus aureus* turned Cellulitis into Osteomyelitis.

To those caregivers at WRH-Met and to those at Hotel-Dieu Grace Hospital that I have failed to mention by name because I was too fevered or drugged or unprepared to record you, *mea maxima culpa*. You have my deepest thanks.

I would be remiss if I didn't thank Calvin Little, Director, Centres for Seniors, Windsor, and staff, for helping Donna through this emotional ordeal and for sending me their best wishes; Erie St. Clair Community Care Access for providing me with medical supplies and medication; Saint Elizabeth Health Care for sending nurses to my home to administer my Vancomycin, and to bandage my surgical wound; Amherstburg Pharma Plus for delivering my medication, pump, and IV supplies to my door; and, Emmanuel A., Pharmacist and Manager, Huda S., Pharmacist, and Carmella N., Pharmacy Assistant, at the Wadland Walker Rd. Pharmacy for their kind wishes.

acknowledgments

When it comes to Donna, best friend, lover, and wife, my heart wells so deeply that words finally fail me, and I am overwhelmed by a deep, abiding, eternal flame.

I wish to thank the Messengers who refused to leave my side during my hospitalization. I am always humbled by your presence. And I thank you for your guidance, inspiration, and love.

Lastly, I wish to thank God for granting me the creativity, tenacity, and vision to fulfill a promise, for sending Messengers to watch over me during the process, and for making a point, at the expense of my *hallux dextra*, to remind me of the great good that some people do every day. I am grateful.

Thank you for reading the Hardcover Edition of *Tellusian Seed* by Mark A. Carter. If you enjoyed reading this novel, you may want to read the book that started it all: *Hephzibah of Heaven*, if you haven't already, and the prequel entitled *Thea of the Seraphim*.

Visit http://markacarter.com to share in the amusing opinions of the author about this and that, to read more about these books, and / or to place an order.

Now you know.

pe cursian

Latost cuman pe cursian.
Maeg pas hwa durran tellan pe
ancien wegs oppe pe halig words
be stricen blind bi pe godas ond
bi eten on life, ofer pe periode aef on wice,
be mapas, wryms, ond other laze formes.

www.ingramcontent.com/pod-product-compliance
Lightning Source LLC
Chambersburg PA
CBHW030417100426
42812CB00028B/2992/J